CHANGING COURSE

A NEW DIRECTION FOR U.S. RELATIONS WITH THE MUSLIM WORLD

Report of the Leadership Group on
U.S.-Muslim Engagement

September 2008

U.S.-Muslim
ENGAGEMENT PROJECT

Washington, DC • Cambridge, MA

First printing, September 2008

Printed in the United States of America on recycled paper containing a minimum of 30% post-consumer content

ISBN 13: 978-0-9797771-7-2

Preface

IN JANUARY 2007, a group of American leaders concerned about the rise in tension and violence between the U.S. and Muslim countries and communities, and interested in finding ways to improve relations, came together to launch the U.S.-Muslim Engagement Project. They were convened by two public consensus-building organizations, Search for Common Ground and the Consensus Building Institute. The group's first meeting took place at the Rockefeller Brothers Fund's Pocantico Conference Center in Tarrytown, New York.

This 34-member, bipartisan Leadership Group includes a former Secretary and a former Deputy Secretary of State; two former members of Congress; a former U.S. Ambassador for the Middle East peace process; a retired Lieutenant General and a former Under Secretary of Defense; Muslim, Christian, and Jewish religious and cultural leaders; philanthropists; business leaders; and experts on foreign and defense policy, public opinion, conflict resolution, and the psychology of extremism.

For nearly two years, the Leadership Group has examined the state of U.S. relations with Muslims around the world, the obstacles to improving relations, how those obstacles could be overcome, and how this project could best contribute to progress. The Leadership Group and project staff have reviewed and discussed the issues with hundreds of counterparts in the U.S. and abroad, and have used polling data and citizen deliberations to explore and test the viability of options for improving relations.

This Report represents a strong consensus among the Leadership Group's members on fundamental principles and core recommendations for improving U.S. relations with Muslim countries and communities, with some variation in support for particular findings and recommendations. Where there are significant differences in the views of Leadership Group members, the Report notes those differences.

While we called our endeavor the "U.S.-Muslim Engagement Project," we acknowledge the challenge of giving it a name that properly reflects our mission. The term "U.S.-Muslim" may imply to some an "us and them" relationship. However, the central thrust of this Report is just the opposite. Its central goal is to show how people across countries, religions, and ethnicities can work in concert to address underlying tensions and reduce the threats that violent extremists pose.

Finally, in both the title of this Report and in the text, there are references to "Muslim countries and communities," "the global Muslim community," "U.S.-Muslim relations," and the "Muslim world." We have used these terms for lack of a better, encompassing reference to the many and diverse Muslim countries and communities in Africa, the Middle East, Asia, Europe, the Americas, and Australia. While there are commonalities across the Muslim world, and a global Muslim community exists in the same sense as a global Christian or Jewish community, any approach to improving "U.S.-Muslim" relations must recognize the great diversity in conditions, cultures, and perspectives among the world's 1.3 billion Muslims. Success in improving our relations requires highly tailored responses to specific issues and opportunities in many different settings.

Search for Common Ground and the Consensus Building Institute, two non-profit organizations with expertise in building consensus on complex public issues, conceived, convened and staffed this project.

The William and Flora Hewlett Foundation, Rockefeller Brothers Fund, Carnegie Corporation of New York, American Petroleum Institute, the Bernard and Audre Rapoport Foundation, the W.K. Kellogg Foundation, One Nation, Mr. George Russell, and other individual and institutional donors have provided major financial and in kind support for the project.

Leadership Group Members*

Madeleine Albright	Principal, The Albright Group LLC; former U.S. Secretary of State
Richard Armitage	President, Armitage International; former U.S. Deputy Secretary of State
Ziad Asali	President and Founder, American Task Force on Palestine
Steve Bartlett	President and Chief Executive Officer, Financial Services Roundtable; former U.S. Representative; former Mayor of Dallas, Texas
Paul Brest	President, The William and Flora Hewlett Foundation

---

* *Organizational affiliations are listed for identification only. Leadership Group members endorse this Report in their personal capacities.*

Paul Brest	President, The William and Flora Hewlett Foundation
Red Cavaney	President and Chief Executive Officer, American Petroleum Institute
Daniel Christman	Lt. General (ret.), U.S. Army; Senior Vice President for International Affairs, U.S. Chamber of Commerce
Stephen Covey	Co-Founder and Vice Chairman, FranklinCovey; writer, speaker, and academic
Thomas Dine	Principal, The Dine Group; former Executive Director, American Israel Public Affairs Committee
Marc Gopin	James H. Laue Professor of World Religions, Diplomacy and Conflict Resolution; Director, Center for World Religions, Diplomacy and Conflict Resolution, Institute for Conflict Analysis and Resolution, George Mason University
Stephen Heintz	President, Rockefeller Brothers Fund
Shamil Idriss	Chairman of the Board, Soliya
Daisy Khan	Executive Director, American Society for Muslim Advancement
Derek Kirkland	Advisory Director, Investment Banking Division, Morgan Stanley
Richard Land	President, The Ethics & Religious Liberty Commission, Southern Baptist Convention; Member, U.S. Commission on International Religious Freedom

Robert Jay Lifton	Lecturer on Psychiatry, Harvard Medical School; author of *Superpower Syndrome*
Denis Madden	Auxiliary Bishop of Baltimore; former Associate Secretary General, Catholic Near East Welfare Association
John Marks	President and Founder, Search for Common Ground
Susan Collin Marks	Senior Vice President, Search for Common Ground; author of *Watching the Wind: Conflict Resolution during South Africa's Transition to Democracy*
Ingrid Mattson	President, The Islamic Society of North America; Professor of Islamic Studies, Director of Islamic Chaplaincy, and Director, Duncan Black Macdonald Center for the Study of Islam and Christian-Muslim Relations, Hartford Seminary
Sayyeda Mirza-Jafri	Strategic Philanthropy Consultant
Dalia Mogahed	Executive Director, Gallup Center for Muslim Studies; co-author with John Esposito of *Who Speaks for Islam? What a Billion Muslims Really Think*
Vali Nasr	Professor of International Politics, The Fletcher School, Tufts University; Adjunct Senior Fellow for Middle Eastern Studies, Council on Foreign Relations
Feisal Abdul Rauf	Imam, Masjid al-Farah in New York City; Founder and Chairman, Cordoba Initiative; author of *What's Right with Islam Is What's Right with America*

Rob Rehg	President, Washington, DC office, Edelman
Dennis Ross	Consultant, Washington Institute for Near East Policy; former U.S. Special Middle East Envoy and Negotiator
S. Abdallah Schleifer	Distinguished Professor of Journalism, American University in Cairo; former Washington Bureau Chief, Al Arabiya news channel; former NBC News Cairo bureau chief
Jessica Stern	Lecturer in Public Policy, Harvard Kennedy School of Government
Mustapha Tlili	Director, Center for Dialogues: Islamic World-U.S.-The West, New York University
William Ury	Co-Founder, Program on Negotiation, Harvard Law School; co-author of *Getting to Yes*
Vin Weber	Managing Partner, Clark and Weinstock; Chairman, National Endowment for Democracy; former U.S. Representative
Daniel Yankelovich	Founder and Chairman, Public Agenda; author
Ahmed Younis	Senior Analyst, Gallup Center for Muslim Studies; former National Director, Muslim Public Affairs Committee
Dov Zakheim	Vice President, Booz Allen Hamilton; former U.S. Under Secretary of Defense (Comptroller)

Contents

If we are to have partners for peace, then we must first be partners in sympathetic recognition that all mankind possesses in common like aspirations and hungers, like ideals and appetites, like purposes and frailties, a like demand for economic advancement. The divisions between us are artificial and transient. Our common humanity is God-made and enduring.

President Dwight D. Eisenhower

Centennial Commencement Address
Pennsylvania State University
June 11, 1955

Executive Summary

CREATING PARTNERSHIPS FOR PEACE with Muslim countries and communities is one of the greatest challenges—and opportunities—facing the United States today. Currently, conflict, misunderstanding, and distrust plague U.S. relations with Muslims in many countries, imperiling security for all. Maintaining the status quo raises the specter of prolonged confrontation, catastrophic attacks, and a cycle of retaliation.

Despite these tensions, the vast majority of Americans and Muslims around the world want peace, amicable relations, good governance, prosperity, and respect. Policies and actions—not a clash of civilizations—are at the root of our divisions.

This Report outlines a comprehensive strategy for the U.S. to enhance international security by improving relations with key Muslim countries and communities. The strategy reflects the consensus of 34 American leaders, including 11 Muslim Americans, in the fields of foreign and defense policy, politics, business, religion, education, public opinion, psychology, philanthropy, and conflict resolution. We come from different walks of life, faiths, political perspectives, and

1

professional disciplines. Our shared goal is to develop and work to implement a wise, widely supportable strategy to make the U.S. and the world safer by responding to the primary causes of tension between the U.S. and Muslims around the world. We believe that a strategy that builds on shared and complementary interests with Muslims in many countries is feasible, desirable, and consistent with core American values.

The central message of our strategy is that the U.S. government, business, faith, education, and media leaders must work with Muslim counterparts to build a coalition that will turn the tide against extremism. Our recommendations are directed primarily to U.S. leaders and institutions, but we can succeed only if counterparts in Muslim majority countries and communities also take responsibility for addressing key challenges: reducing extremism, resolving political and sectarian conflicts, holding governments accountable, creating more vibrant economies, correcting misconceptions, and engaging in dialogue to build mutual respect and understanding.

The Need for a New Approach

During the past several years, it has become clear that military force may be necessary, but is not sufficient, to defeat violent extremists in Iraq, Afghanistan, and Pakistan, or to prevent attacks elsewhere. Moreover, military action has significant costs to U.S. standing in the world, and to our ability to gain the cooperation of other countries in counterterrorism and counterinsurgency operations. Senior U.S. defense and military leaders have recognized the primary importance of diplomatic, political, economic, and cultural initiatives in combating extremism.

Recently, the U.S. government has taken important steps to expand the use of diplomacy, support improvements in governance, and promote economic development in Muslim countries threatened by extremism. In the face of continuing extremist violence directed at the U.S. and its allies, the next U.S. President and Congress must create and implement a more comprehensive strategy for reversing extremism in key Muslim regions, countries, and communities. U.S. business, educational, philanthropic, faith, and media organizations should help define and carry out many elements of that strategy.

The Drivers of Extremism

[handwritten annotations: Active-vs-Passive Support; We have to make Passive Support React Negatively; Against extremists]

Only a tiny minority of Muslims is involved in violence against the U.S. and its allies. The extremists' ability to recruit, operate, and inflict harm depends on a more widespread set of active and passive supporters. In many Muslim majority countries and Muslim minority communities, that support is driven by deep-seated frustration with poor governance, constraints on political activity, and lack of economic opportunity.

The United States is not directly responsible for these conditions and frustrations, but many Muslims see the U.S. as complicit, believing that it has supported ineffective and corrupt governments in their countries as a way to meet U.S. geopolitical and economic interests. Their anger is compounded by their sense that the U.S. has favored Israel in its conflict with the Palestinians, and has exercised a "double standard" on democracy, calling for democratic reforms in the Muslim world while continuing to support repressive governments in allied Muslim countries. Since the invasion of Iraq, many Muslims have also come to believe that the U.S. seeks to dominate Muslim countries by force. Efforts by the U.S. government, private leaders and organizations to change these perceptions have had limited effect.

A Strategy for Reversing Extremism

To shrink the base of support for extremism, our strategy calls on U.S. governmental and private leaders, and their Muslim counterparts, to work together to advance four goals: resolving conflicts through diplomacy; improving governance in Muslim countries; promoting broad-based economic development in Muslim countries and regions; and building mutual respect and understanding.

Efforts on each of these goals will be helpful, but coordinated action on all four goals, tailored to particular countries and regions, offers the greatest potential for improvements in U.S. security and U.S.-Muslim relations. Following is a summary of our recommendations for advancing each of the four goals.

1. Elevate diplomacy as the primary tool for resolving key conflicts involving Muslim countries, engaging both allies and adversaries in dialogue

- Engage with Iran to explore the potential for agreements that could increase regional security, while seeking Iran's full compliance with its nuclear nonproliferation commitments

- Work intensively for immediate de-escalation of the Israeli-Palestinian conflict and a viable path to a two-state solution, while ensuring the security of Israelis and Palestinians

- Promote broad-based political reconciliation in Iraq, and clarify the long-term U.S. role

- Renew international commitment and cooperation to halt extremists' resurgence in Afghanistan and Pakistan

- Provide top-level U.S. leadership to resolve regional conflicts and to improve coordination with international partners

2. Support efforts to improve governance and promote civic participation in Muslim countries, and advocate for principles rather than parties in their internal political contests

- Build the capacity of government institutions to deliver services, and of citizens to participate in governance

- Advocate consistently for nonviolence, pluralism and fairness in political contests

- Use U.S. leverage with authoritarian governments to promote reforms in governance

- Assess the value of engagement with political representatives of armed and activist movements case-by-case, based on their principles, behavior, and level of public support

- Support political transitions and the consolidation of reforms in countries at critical "turning points"

3. Help catalyze job-creating growth in Muslim countries to benefit both the U.S. and Muslim countries' economies

- Support policy reforms to secure property rights, facilitate transactions and promote investments

- Partner with governments, multilateral institutions and philanthropies to make education a more powerful engine of employment and entrepreneurship

- Use public-private investment partnerships to reduce risk, promote exports and fund enterprises

- Use trade agreements to reward economic reform and spur investment

- Manage energy interdependence and diversify resources

4. Improve mutual respect and understanding between Americans and Muslims around the world

- Use public diplomacy to reinforce changes in policies and actions

- Dramatically expand cross-cultural education, people-to-people and interfaith exchange

- Promote greater depth and accuracy in news coverage and programming

- Invest in cultural diplomacy through arts and entertainment programs, to deepen mutual understanding and challenge stereotypes

- Involve the Muslim-American community as a bridge

A Call for Action

Implementing this strategy will require a sustained, coordinated effort by a range of public and private institutions, including the President and Executive agencies; Members of Congress; business and investment leaders; philanthropic institutions and development agencies; and educators, faith leaders, the news media, and citizens.

The next U.S. President and Administration must provide immediate and sustained leadership to improve U.S.-Muslim relations. We recommend that the next President take these steps:

- Speak to the critical importance of improving relations with the global Muslim community in his 2009 inaugural address

- Take key actions immediately to demonstrate a commitment to improving relations, including:

  - Immediately organizing a whole-of-government effort, with Presidential leadership, to define and implement a strategy for improving relations with key Muslim countries and communities

  - Immediately re-affirming the U.S. commitment to prohibit all forms of torture

- Within the first three months of the Administration, initiate a major and sustained diplomatic effort to resolve regional conflicts and promote security cooperation in the Middle East, giving top priority to engagement with Iran and permanent resolution of the Israeli-Palestinian conflict

- Within the first six months of the Administration, co-convene a business-government summit on economic reform, growth, and job creation in the Middle East to accelerate current reform and investment initiatives

- Work with leaders in Congress, educational, cultural and philanthropic institutions in the U.S., and counterparts in Muslim countries, to create and fund a global initiative for teaching, learning, and exchange among citizens in the U.S. and Muslim countries

It will also be important for a wide range of private actors to coordinate their activities more closely, while maintaining their separation from the government. To do so, we recommend that the new Administration and leading business, educational, philanthropic, faith, and media organizations co-convene forums on U.S.-Muslim relations, and create new platforms for action, making special efforts to involve Muslim-American leaders.

What Is at Stake

Immediate action is needed. Neither the U.S. nor Muslims in regions of conflict can afford a further deterioration in relations. Extremist groups and movements have gained ground in many Muslim countries. Their appeal will grow unless the U.S. acts more effectively to address the economic, political, and security concerns that extremists have exploited.

Implementing our recommendations will not eliminate the risk of terrorist attacks affecting the U.S. Yet given a broad, deep, and sustained commitment, our proposed strategy will reshape U.S. relations with Muslim leaders and peoples in ways that improve U.S. and international security, transform the spiral of fear and mistrust into a foundation of mutual confidence and respect, and help create a more peaceful world.

The Leadership Group on U.S -Muslim Engagement
September 2008

I.

Introduction

IMPROVING RELATIONS WITH MUSLIM majority countries and communities is one of the most important foreign policy and national security challenges facing the United States. In the wake of the September 11, 2001 terrorist attacks, the U.S. sought to strengthen its own security. Despite our leaders' insistence that we had no conflict with Islam or Muslims, and despite a long history of U.S. action to protect and aid Muslims affected by war or natural disaster, our responses to 9/11 have sparked fear, mistrust, and hostility among many Muslims. Antipathy toward the U.S. has risen not only in the countries most directly affected by U.S. military action (Iraq, Afghanistan, Iran, and Pakistan), but in many others around the world. In turn, violent extremist groups that claim to act in the name of Islam have used the climate of distrust to gain support for further attacks on U.S. assets and allies. Though majorities in both the U.S. and Muslim countries around the world want to reverse this spiral of violence, many fear that it will continue to escalate.

The extremists who seek to harm and destroy the U.S. represent a very small minority of Muslims, operating, for the most part, independent of governments, through loose networks of social, financial, and logistical support. Given their strong convictions, and the limited ability of the U.S. and its allies to identify and target them, they are difficult to dissuade or deter. Were an extremist group to use a nuclear, chemical, or biological weapon, or sabotage a hazardous facility in a populated area in the U.S., it could kill tens of thousands or more.[1]

This Report begins with the premise that the U.S. must work with Muslim counterparts who share our interest in improving mutual security to minimize the risk of such a scenario. Responsibility for peaceful coexistence rests equally with U.S. and Muslim leaders worldwide.

For the U.S., counterterrorism operations are a necessary part of the strategy to keep Americans safe. However, these operations treat the symptoms rather than the causes of conflict. There is a deep reservoir of grievances against the U.S. among Muslims around the world. Whether or not these grievances are justified, the climate of hostility makes it possible for extremist groups to recruit and operate with relative ease in many countries and communities. To reduce the risk of conflict, now and in the future, the U.S. must not only defend itself against attacks, but also build more positive relations with key countries and counterparts across the Muslim world.

Today, the U.S. stands at a crossroads in its relations with the global Muslim community. There is still a strong set of shared values and interests among American and Muslim leaders and publics. Together, we can rebuild trust and address the core causes of tension. There are numerous diplomatic, political, economic, and people-to-people initiatives on which to build. But if we continue on our current course, time is not on our side.

The U.S. government, in concert with business, faith, education, and civic leaders, needs to undertake major initiatives to address the

---

1 Recent expert estimates of the likelihood that a terrorist group will successfully detonate a nuclear weapon in a U.S. or European city within the next 10 years have a mid-range of 30 percent to 50 percent. Some experts consider the risk to be substantially higher and others, substantially lower. See Michael Levi and Graham Allison, discussants, "How Likely is a Nuclear Terrorist Attack on the United States?" Council on Foreign Relations, April 2007. Numerous U.S. hazardous facilities in populated areas remain vulnerable to attack. See Stephen Flynn, "The Next Attack," *Washington Monthly*, March 2007.

causes of tension. Working with Muslim counterparts, we can achieve substantial joint gains in peace and security, political and economic development, and respect and understanding.

The alternative is to increase our reliance on military action and counterterrorism in alliance with unpopular authoritarian governments. Doing so will raise the risk that our worst fears will be realized. For the sake of our own national security, values, and aspirations, and those of more than a billion Muslims around the world, we must forge a new approach.

The Leadership Group and the U.S.-Muslim Engagement Project

This Report presents the consensus of 34 American leaders in the fields of foreign and defense policy, politics, business, religion, education, public opinion, psychology, philanthropy, and conflict resolution. We come from different walks of life, faiths, political perspectives, and professional disciplines. Our shared goal is to develop and work to implement a wise, widely supportable strategy to make the U.S. and the world safer, by responding to the primary causes of tension with Muslims around the world. We believe that a strategy that builds on shared and complementary interests with Muslims in many countries is feasible, desirable, and consistent with core American values.

The Report also reflects dialogue with hundreds of American leaders and counterparts in Muslim countries, and research on the views of millions of citizens in the U.S. and in Muslim countries whose perspectives and preferences we have explored. We have used the process of dialogue and public opinion research not only to build a leadership consensus, but also to craft a strategy that can win broad public and political support in the U.S., and build partnerships with Muslim leaders and people across the world.

This project was convened, facilitated, and supported by two organizations with expertise in building consensus on difficult public issues: Search for Common Ground and the Consensus Building Institute. In addition, more than a dozen foundations, corporations and individuals have generously funded our work.

II.

Why Are U.S. Relations with Muslim Countries and Communities Important?

U.S. RELATIONS WITH MUSLIM COUNTRIES and communities are critically important for several reasons: the size of the global Muslim population; the geopolitical significance of key Muslim countries and regions; the persistence of conflict in these strategically important regions over several decades; the dramatic rise in tension and violence between the U.S. and a number of Muslim countries and groups during the past decade, and the risk of further conflict escalation; and the potential for both the U.S. and Muslim countries to prosper from improved relations and new partnerships.

Roughly one-fifth of the world's population, or about 1.3 billion people, is Muslim. Muslims form the majority in 56 countries across North Africa; the Middle East; Asia Minor; and Central, South and Southeast Asia.[1] That geography spans major oil producing regions,

---

1   Oxford Islamic Studies Online, "Where do most Muslims live?" available at www.oxfordislamicstudies.com. Contrary to American public perceptions, only 20 percent of the global Muslim population is Arab, and more Muslims live in South and Southeast Asia than in North Africa and the Middle East.

key land and sea trade routes, and areas of high political sensitivity and instability. Muslims also form important minority communities in countries across Europe, North America, Sub-Saharan Africa, Australia, and parts of Asia.

As with all major religious and ethnic communities, there is great diversity in beliefs, values, cultures, political systems, and living standards among the world's Muslim communities. Given this broad range of circumstances and the equally broad range of U.S. interests and relations with Muslim countries, Muslims' views about U.S. policy have traditionally varied widely. There is, however, a clear trend.

Since the 1940s, and more rapidly since the first Gulf War in the early 1990s, more Muslims have become concerned about the U.S. role in supporting authoritarian governments. More have become angry at the U.S. and its allies for their presence in Muslim lands. More feel resentful over the U.S. role in the Israeli-Palestinian conflict, and more feel humiliated by the sense that Americans do not understand or respect Islamic values or cultures. During the past six years, this set of concerns has become even more widespread, consistent and intense. Today, the U.S. faces an extraordinarily strong and widely shared set of negative perceptions among Muslim peoples and their leaders.[2]

From a security standpoint, the primary U.S. focus is on armed extremist groups in Iraq, Pakistan, Afghanistan, Iran, Lebanon, Syria, and Palestine.[3] However, the U.S. must also consider how our policies and actions in those countries, their neighbors, and other Muslim countries around the world shape the ability of extremists to recruit, operate and destabilize governments and societies. Addressing not only the immediate threat of terrorist and insurgent groups, but also their broader bases of support and sympathy, should be a top national priority for four reasons:

---

2   Majorities in Latin America, Western Europe, the former Soviet Union, and parts of Asia also have far less favorable views of the U.S. today. It is important to note that the U.S. government is perceived less favorably than the American people. See Pew Global Attitudes Project, *Rising Environmental Concern in 47-Nation Survey: Global Unease With Major World Powers,* Pew Research Center, June 27, 2007, pp. 13-28.

3   Armed extremists in Algeria, Somalia, and Eritrea are also a significant security concern.

- Muslim public hostility toward the U.S. is generating resources, recruits, and operational opportunities for extremist groups that seek to harm the U.S., its allies, and assets. It is also undermining mainstream Muslim leaders who seek tolerance, nonviolence, and constructive change in relations with the U.S.[4]

- Most Muslims' primary grievances and concerns are about "what the U.S. does," rather than "who we are." At the same time, the U.S. has options for meeting its own interests in ways that are more compatible with most Muslims' interests and values. It is possible to change our relationships to enhance mutual security, meet shared and complementary political goals, generate joint economic gains, and demonstrate mutual respect for each others' core values.

- By adopting a comprehensive strategy and implementing it now, it is likely that the U.S. can significantly change perceptions and behavior among mainstream and politically activist Muslims in key countries before attitudes and beliefs become "locked in" for a generation. On the other hand, failure to act soon will likely lead to a hardening of attitudes, reinforcing extremists' claims that violent resistance to the U.S. is the best path to autonomy, respect, and justice.

- Fighting a long-term conflict with extremists in many Muslim countries will demand continued sacrifice from the U.S. military, carry high economic costs, continue the political acrimony that has divided the country for the past several years, and require the U.S. to use much of its international political capital to maintain alliances. As a result, the U.S. will have fewer resources to address pressing needs at home or other critical challenges abroad.

---

4   Though the vast majority of Muslims do not support acts of violence against civilians, many Muslims currently see attacks on U.S. military targets, and on governments allied to the U.S., as legitimate. See Steven Kull et al., *Muslim Public Opinion on US Policy, Attacks on Civilians and al Qaeda*, World Public Opinion, Program on International Policy Attitudes, University of Maryland (PIPA), April 24, 2007.

It is imperative to change our strategy now. The incoming Administration has a window of opportunity during its first year to make a significant change in course. The strategy we recommend—to make more effective use of diplomacy, development, and dialogue—can improve U.S.-Muslim relations, and produce more security and prosperity. But immediate action is essential.

III

Guiding Principles for Improving U.S.-Muslim Relations

SEVERAL CORE PRINCIPLES and assumptions underpin our assessments and recommendations for improving U.S.-Muslim relations.

It Is Possible for Americans and Muslims Around the World to Live Together Peacefully

Public opinion research clearly shows that majorities of Americans (including millions of Muslims who are deeply integrated into American society and contribute to its vibrancy) and Muslims in other countries have many interests and values in common. They abhor violence and desire to live in peace. They want to pursue economic and political opportunity. And they desire other nations and people to respect them and their religious belief.

The wide range of beliefs and practices across the global Muslim community, and within the U.S., undercut the claim that we are facing an inevitable "clash of civilizations." There are real and important differences on many specific issues, and on some cultural values (though there is great cultural diversity among Muslim societies, as there is within U.S. society). Yet none of our political or cultural differences pose an insurmountable barrier to peaceful coexistence. In fact, the overwhelming majority of victims of Muslim extremist violence are Muslims, and there is a strong, shared interest in ending the use of violence to achieve political goals.

Specific policy changes and actions, combined with new partnerships based on mutual respect and trust, are crucial to reversing the downward spiral in U.S relations with Muslim countries and communities. The goal of our strategy is to build new partnerships that marginalize extremists, improve our mutual security and contribute to peace and prosperity. The evidence that peaceful conflict resolution can succeed across and within nations is all around us: the European Union's deep integration of former deadly foes; the transition from apartheid to multiracial democracy in South Africa; the resolution of Central America's generation-long civil wars; and the end of violent conflict in Northern Ireland, among others.

Leaders in the U.S. and in Muslim Countries Share Responsibility for Transforming Relations

This Report focuses on changes in policy and action by the U.S. But action by the U.S. alone will not produce fundamental shifts in relations. Political, religious, business, and civic leaders in Muslim countries must take responsibility for curbing extremism, promoting economic development, and expanding political participation. They too must work to dispel misconceptions of the U.S. and to promote tolerance. The U.S. can and should work with counterparts in Muslim countries and communities, while recognizing that Muslims must take the lead in addressing conflicts within their societies and communities.

Partnerships Among Leaders and Institutions Worldwide Are Critical to Achieving Change

Though there are some actions that public and private leaders in

Western and Muslim countries can take unilaterally, many initiatives to resolve conflict, support political reform and economic opportunity, and enhance mutual respect and understanding can only succeed if they are created and carried out in coordination or jointly. Partnership can take many forms: exchanges of ideas, commitment of resources, coordinated diplomatic or political action, and people-to-people exchanges, among others.

Partnership does not have to mean a highly visible role for the U.S. There will be situations in which it is more appropriate for U.S. public and private institutions to play a supporting role through multilateral organizations and initiatives. More consistent American participation in international organizations that include Muslim countries could help not only in the direct pursuit of shared objectives, but also in reversing a widespread international perception that the U.S. has disengaged from multilateral organizations that it once helped to lead.

Understanding and Engaging Our Critics and Adversaries Is in Our Interest

There may be times when it is unwise or unworkable to engage with those who have declared themselves our enemies. Nonetheless, we urge both U.S. and Muslim political leaders to err on the side of outreach and inclusion, with flexibility to use official and unofficial channels, public and confidential communication, to explore the potential for constructive dialogue. A commitment to listen to and understand our critics does not require us to accept their legitimacy or meet their goals. Yet only by understanding their aspirations and concerns can we determine whether there are ways to meet both their interests and our own.

The U.S. Has Greater Impact When We Live Up to Our Own Ideals

For much of the world, the U.S. has long been a model of democratic practice, respect for the rule of law, and human rights. When we act in ways clearly inconsistent with our own founding principles and with the human rights we have championed, we spark cynicism and resistance. When our actions are consistent with our ideals, and we offer our economic, political, and cultural assets without imposing them, we can have a powerful and positive impact on leaders and publics in Muslim majority countries and across the world.

The U.S. is already applying our ideals in engagements with Muslims on multiple fronts, including disaster relief (earning public recognition and gratitude in Indonesia after the 2004 tsunami and Pakistan after the 2005 earthquake); private-sector-led economic development (as Coca-Cola has demonstrated in its bottling and distribution operations in the West Bank); advancement of health care (several American medical schools are partnering with Persian Gulf counterparts to establish new medical centers and schools); and the actions of thousands of prominent Americans—including Muslim-Americans--who are engaging in dialogue to promote mutual respect and moderate behavior.

In sum, these five principles provide background to the analysis and set of recommendations that follow, and will remain a touchstone for the Leadership Group as we work together to promote the adoption of a new strategy for U.S.-Muslim engagement.

IV.

The Current State of U.S.-Muslim Relations

THE CONFLICT WITH MUSLIM EXTREMISTS and widespread Muslim frustration with the U.S. did not begin on 9/11. Since the end of World War II, the U.S. has played an increasingly important and sometimes controversial role in Muslim countries across North Africa, the Middle East, and Asia. Though the U.S. did not have a single policy or strategy for relations with Muslim countries, three U.S. interests have been significant in shaping relations:

- Creating and maintaining alliances with Muslim governments to contain Soviet influence

- Maintaining the stability and security of Middle East oil production and supply

- Supporting the state of Israel while seeking intermittently to resolve the Arab-Israeli conflict

Given U.S. concerns, the Middle East has been a major focus of U.S. policy and strategy through the postwar period. Other predominantly Muslim regions and countries gained attention when they became flashpoints in the Cold War conflict (for example, Afghanistan and Pakistan after the 1979 Soviet invasion of Afghanistan). In the brief interval between the end of the Cold War and 9/11, the U.S. sought to aid Muslims in the Balkans and Somalia, while stepping back from some of its Cold War commitments in Afghanistan and the Middle East.[1]

For most Americans, however, U.S.-Muslim relations only came into sharp focus on 9/11. On that day, nearly 3,000 U.S. citizens were killed in attacks carried out by Muslim extremists affiliated with al-Qaeda.

Extremist Threats

Understanding and reducing the threat of further attacks by al-Qaeda and its affiliates is a top priority for the U.S. and many other countries. Al-Qaeda is a loosely organized network of Muslim extremist groups that use violence as a primary means of advancing their goals.[2] It has a very small base of active supporters, and a much larger audience of Muslims who oppose its use of violence against civilians, but who share its goal of resisting what they see as U.S. domination and aggression

---

1   An Annex at the end of this Report presents a brief historical sketch of U.S.-Muslim relations since the end of World War II.

2   The use of the term "terrorist groups" to refer to al-Qaeda, its affiliates, and supporters may not be the most useful starting point for analysis or the development of strategy. Lt. Col. David Kilcullen, currently a senior advisor to the U.S. military in Iraq, has offered an alternative assessment of this network as a "global insurgency," and has proposed a strategy of "disaggregation," integrating a wide range of civil, political, economic, and diplomatic tools, as a way to limit the network's reach and impact. See David Kilcullen, "Countering Global Insurgency," *Journal of Strategic Studies* 28, no. 4 (2005). David C. Gompert, John Gordon IV et al. make a similar argument, framing the current challenge primarily as a set of linked "global-local insurgencies," in Chapter 2 of *War by Other Means: Building Complete and Balanced Capabilities for Counterinsurgency* (Santa Monica: RAND Corporation, 2008). The Leadership Group recognizes the value of counterinsurgency doctrine for the U.S. military and civil-military planning contexts, and we have incorporated many similar and complementary elements in our strategy. Yet there is at least one important conceptual difference: we see improving relations as the long-term goal, and counterinsurgency as a means to advancing that goal.

in the Muslim world.[3] Before 9/11, al-Qaeda's leaders declared that Muslims around the world have a duty to oppose the U.S., because it has acted contrary to the values and interests of Muslim peoples. Their indictment of the U.S. was based on several claims: the U.S. had established military bases in Muslim regions as a means of domination; the U.S. supported Israeli occupation of Palestinian territories; and the U.S. supported corrupt governments in the Middle East and elsewhere in the Muslim world.[4] Since 9/11, al-Qaeda has used the U.S. invasion of Iraq, the continuing Israeli-Palestinian conflict, and the Taliban insurgency in Afghanistan as rallying points.

Though a large majority of Muslims globally condemns the 9/11 attacks on the U.S., and even larger majorities in many Muslim countries oppose all violence against civilians, al-Qaeda, its affiliates, and its imitators continue to draw recruits from a global reservoir of young Muslims.[5] Some recruits feel alienated and under attack in their own communities. Others identify with Muslims in other parts of the world whom they see as victims of U.S. policies, alliances, and actions.[6]

The Global War on Terror

Since 9/11, Americans have faced a new, global challenge: how to

3   See Dalia Mogahed, "Muslims and Americans: The Way Forward," Gallup Center for Muslim World Studies, 2006, and Steven Kull, Director, Program on International Policy Attitudes, University of Maryland, "Negative Attitudes toward the United States in the Muslim World: Do They Matter?" Testimony to the U.S. House of Representatives, Committee on Foreign Affairs, Subcommittee on International Organizations, Human Rights, and Oversight, May 17, 2007, available at www.worldpublicopinion.org.

4   "Jihad Against Jews and Crusaders," World Islamic Front Statement, February 23, 1998, available online from the Federation of American Scientists at www.fas.org.

5   Information on opposition to the 9/11 attacks from John Esposito and Dalia Mogahed, *Who Speaks for Islam? What a Billion Muslims Really Think* (Washington, DC: Gallup Press, 2008), p. 69. See also the authors' response to the question "How did you define the 'politically radicalized' and 'moderates'?" on the Gallup Web site at www.gallup.com. Statistics on majorities opposing violence against civilians from Kull, "Negative Attitudes," op. cit.

6   See e.g. Marc Sageman, *Leaderless Jihad: Terror Networks in the Twenty-First Century* (Philadelphia: University of Pennsylvania Press, 2008). The Leadership Group notes that there is a need for continuing research on the factors driving radicalization and recruitment to Muslim extremist groups.

prevent further attacks by al-Qaeda and other Muslim extremist groups while rebuilding good relations with Muslim countries and communities. To date, the main U.S. strategy has been to pursue a Global War on Terror (GWOT). This effort has focused on counterterrorism actions around the world, regime change in Afghanistan and Iraq, containment of Iran's government, and intensified economic and military support for governments considered allies in operations against al-Qaeda, its affiliates, and its imitators.

According to the July 2007 National Intelligence Estimate on al-Qaeda from the U.S. intelligence community, the GWOT disrupted al-Qaeda's leadership temporarily. However, al-Qaeda is rebuilding itself, and has spawned a more loosely connected network of like-minded extremist groups.[7] Recent reports from the Central Intelligence Agency (CIA) indicate that the continuing campaign against al-Qaeda and affiliates in Pakistan, Iraq, and Saudi Arabia has done serious damage to its operations. However, there is ongoing, vigorous debate on al-Qaeda's capacities. An August 2008 intelligence assessment suggests that al-Qaeda has regained the capacity to conduct major operations.[8]

In Iraq, despite a marked reduction in violence and political progress on some divisive issues (for example, reintegration of Baathists and scheduling provincial elections), the current government has not been able to create a stable constitutional agreement among the country's major ethnic groups and sects. A multiparty insurgency continues to attack the U.S. and its allies. Iraq has become a training ground in political violence for Muslim extremists, and its continuing unrest has further destabilized the Middle East. Afghanistan has a new government committed in principle to pluralism and economic development,

---

7   See U.S. National Intelligence Council, "National Intelligence Estimate: The Terrorist Threat to the US Homeland," July 2007.

8   See Joby Warrick, "U.S. Claims Big Gains Against Al Qaeda," *Washington Post,* May 30, 2008. See also the statement of Ted Gistaro, U.S. National Intelligence Officer for Transnational Threats, at the Washington Institute for Near East Policy, August 12, 2008, available at www.washington-institute.org, indicating that "in spite of successful U.S. and allied operations against al-Qaeda, especially the death of important al-Qaeda figures since December, the group has maintained or strengthened key elements of its capability to attack the United States in the past year."

but has not yet achieved political stability or economic improvements in the lives of most citizens.

The U.S. has increased military and economic aid not only to the new governments of Afghanistan and Iraq, but also to key allied governments in the Muslim world, most notably in Egypt, Jordan, Saudi Arabia, Pakistan, and Indonesia. Most of these governments have problematic political and human rights records. While seeking their help against extremist groups, the U.S. has also intermittently urged the leaders of these countries to liberalize their political systems and uphold human rights, with very limited success.

Muslim Perceptions of the GWOT and the U.S.

The net impact of U.S. actions after 9/11 on Muslim public opinion has been strikingly negative, according to the best available public opinion research. Substantial majorities of Muslims outside the U.S. now have much less favorable views of the U.S. (as do the publics in many Western countries). The main reason for these negative views is *not* a dislike for American values. On the contrary, most Muslims admire the same things about America and the West that Americans do: technology and economic progress, the work ethic, and political freedoms; and they want similar economic and political opportunities.[9]

Public opinion analysis indicates that the main drivers of Muslim public antipathy to the U.S. are widely shared concerns about U.S. policies and actions. Majorities in many Muslim countries believe that the U.S. seeks political domination in Muslim regions (through its support for authoritarian governments in Muslim countries and its military presence); disrespects Islam as a religion; and is fueling violent conflicts whose primary victims are Muslims, particularly through its direct occupation of Iraq and its perceived support for Israeli occupation of Palestinian territories. Many Muslims also hold the U.S. at

---

9   See Esposito and Mogahed, *Who Speaks for Islam?* op. cit., pp. 80-81. For ongoing polling of the global Muslim population on issues in politics and culture, see the Muslim-West Facts Initiative, at www.muslimwestfacts.com.

least partly responsible for limits on their own political and economic opportunities.[10]

The Diversity of Muslim Concerns

Though the global data are significant, it is important to clarify the diversity of Muslim concerns, and to understand how national and regional circumstances shape those concerns. Our analysis[11] suggests that we can best understand the range of Muslim political perceptions as a pyramid:

- A large base of *mainstream* Muslims who make up 90-95 percent of the population in nearly all Muslim majority countries, with the highest proportions in Southeast Asia and North Africa

- A much smaller percentage of *politically activist* who make up 5-10 percent of the population in most countries, but with proportions up to 25 percent in conflict-affected countries (Palestine, Iraq, Iran, Afghanistan, and Pakistan), and in the neighboring states of Egypt, Jordan, Lebanon, Syria, and Saudi Arabia

- An extremely small number (on the order of 0.01 percent globally) of active *insurgents and extremists* who use violence, concentrated in the conflict-affected countries, with small cells scattered across the rest of the world[12]

---

10   PIPA, "Global Poll Finds that Religion and Culture are Not to Blame for Tensions between Islam and the West," February 16, 2007. See also Kurt M. Campbell and Richard Weitz, *Non-Military Strategies for Countering Islamist Terrorism: Lessons Learned from Past Counterinsurgencies* (Princeton, N.J.: Princeton Project on National Security, 2005).

11   The primary sources for analysis are the series of polls by PIPA, Pew, and Gallup cited earlier. The "pyramid" description presented here is a refinement of the available information, drawing particularly—though not exclusively—on the Gallup data referenced in Esposito and Mogahed, *Who Speaks for Islam?* op. cit. The pyramid description should not be taken as a definitive portrait of Muslim public opinion, which is fluid and responsive to changes in the national and international context. Nevertheless, it is a useful starting point for understanding the diversity of Muslim concerns and the potential for different kinds of action by the U.S. to address those concerns.

12   One expert estimate puts the total number of armed insurgents at approximately 200,000, of

In broad terms, *mainstream* Muslims are primarily concerned about their economic prospects, secondarily about good governance and political accountability in their own countries. They may want greater U.S. support for economic and political reform in their own countries, and may be angry and frustrated with what they perceive as U.S. aggression in the areas of conflict, but they do not support extremists and want to reduce their influence globally and in their own countries. Some of the most populous Muslim countries have the highest percentages of mainstream Muslims.

The *politically activist* have similar concerns, but they place higher priority on political reform than economic opportunity, and are more likely to want governance based solely on Islamic principles (that is, on their interpretation of *Sharia*). Many are so outraged by what they perceive as U.S. support for authoritarian governments, and by U.S. military and counterterrorism operations that harm Muslims in their own and other countries, that they believe insurgent and terrorist violence is justified in some cases. A fraction of the politically activist participates in radical politics. On average, people with this belief set are somewhat younger, better educated, and have higher incomes than mainstream Muslims.

The *insurgents and extremists* include those fighting the U.S. and its allies in Iraq, Afghanistan, and Pakistan, and in cells elsewhere. They are willing to use violence as a primary means of political change in their own and other countries, to overturn what they see as illegitimate governments, and to force the U.S. to withdraw from Muslim lands. Though both insurgent and extremist groups may attack civilian as well as military targets, it is very important to differentiate their goals. Insurgent groups in Iraq and Afghanistan are fighting locally for national or ethnic self-determination. Their primary targets tend to be military forces and political opponents, though insurgents in Iraq have carried out large-scale attacks on civilians.

Transnational extremist movements, including al-Qaeda and its

---

whom no more than a few thousand are transnational extremists. See Campbell and Weitz, *Non-Military Strategies for Countering Islamist Terrorism,* op. cit.

affiliates, are fighting for a broader set of political and social transformations, to eject the U.S. and the West from all Muslim lands, and establish states based on their interpretations of Islamic principles. Extremists' demographic profile is varied, but al-Qaeda's leaders have levels of education and family income similar to the politically activist group.[13]

Strident misrepresentations of U.S. actions and intentions by Osama bin Laden and other extremist leaders, along with polarizing media coverage, have undoubtedly contributed to the climate of public anger across the Muslim world. Nonetheless, many Muslims with a sophisticated understanding of the U.S. and the world, and generally moderate political views, are deeply angered by the negative impacts of the GWOT. They sympathize with the causes for which al-Qaeda and affiliated terrorists claim to be fighting, though they condemn al-Qaeda's methods.[14]

Despite deep and widespread frustration with the U.S., it is important to note a countervailing key fact: majorities and pluralities in many Muslim countries would like relations with the U.S. to improve.[15]

U.S. Public Perceptions of Relations with Muslims

In the U.S., more than 75 percent of the American public is worried that the U.S. is on the wrong track in its relations with Muslim countries.[16] Most Americans are concerned about violent extremism across the Muslim world, though they admit to ignorance of Muslim countries and people. Thirty-three percent of Americans say that there is

---

13 The 9/11 attackers, for example, were almost all middle class. See Lawrence Wright, *The Looming Tower: Al Qaeda and the Road to 9/11* (New York: Knopf, 2006).

14 See for example Craig Charney and Nicole Yakatan, *A New Beginning: Strategies for a More Fruitful Dialogue with the Muslim World,* CSR No. 7, May 2005 (New York: Council on Foreign Relations, 2005).

15 Dalia Mogahed, "The Current State of U.S. Relations with the Muslim World: A Data-driven Analysis," presentation to the Leadership Group on U.S.-Muslim Engagement, using Gallup Organization Muslim world polling data, January 2007. See also Mogahed, "Muslims and Americans: The Way Forward," op. cit.

16 Public Agenda and *Foreign Affairs,* "Confidence in U.S. Foreign Policy Index," Spring 2008, esp. p. 19 for worries on hatred of the U.S. in Muslim countries, Islamist extremism rising, U.S. action in the Middle East aiding terrorist recruitment, and potential for further terrorist attacks.

nothing they admire about Muslim societies, and 25 percent say that they do not know enough to have an opinion.[17]

To defend against the hatred and violence of terrorists and extremists, the public strongly supports improving U.S. intelligence, making the U.S. less dependent on oil from the Middle East, and tightening restrictions on immigration. Majorities also believe that U.S. action in Iraq and our counterterrorism strategy are angering Muslims, and want the U.S. to make greater use of diplomacy and dialogue with our critics and adversaries, including Iran and Syria. However, there is little public support for advocating democracy or increasing foreign aid. The public is uncertain whether any other actions could be more effective in improving relations.[18]

---

17   Mogahed, "The Current State of U.S. Relations with the Muslim World: A Data-driven Analysis," op. cit.

18   See Public Agenda and *Foreign Affairs,* "Confidence in U.S. Foreign Policy Index," Spring 2008, op. cit., esp. p. 20 for views on strategies. See also PIPA, "Americans Believe U.S. International Strategy Has Backfired," December 6, 2006, and PIPA, "US Role in the World," 2007.

V.

A New Strategy for U.S.-Muslim Relations

TODAY, THE U.S. STILL FACES the basic challenge it confronted after 9/11: preventing further attacks by al-Qaeda and other Muslim extremist groups while addressing the underlying sources of tension.

A substantial majority of the American public, and a number of policy makers and analysts, now have serious concerns about the GWOT as the primary strategy for ensuring U.S. security and promoting good relations with Muslims. Specific criticisms of the GWOT are that it has focused too much attention on Iraq, with serious consequences for U.S. relations with many other countries; has not focused enough on destroying al-Qaeda's leadership (widely believed to be hiding in the borderlands between Pakistan and Afghanistan); has not increased U.S. intelligence capacity enough to consistently detect and disrupt Muslim extremist cells and terrorist plans; has undermined the image and stature of the U.S. in the Muslim world (and among many traditional U.S. allies in the West) by violating legal protections for Muslims suspected of links to extremist groups; and has not effectively addressed the underlying grievances that are generating widespread Muslim public hostility to the U.S.[1]

In response, U.S. defense and military leaders and analysts are developing new strategies and doctrines for dealing with what some have called "a global insurgency." At the core of their thinking is a much greater emphasis on the non-military components of strategy: strengthening the legitimacy and governance capacity of governments threatened by extremism and helping them improve economic conditions; and making much greater use of diplomatic and political tools to resolve conflicts. With these components in place, they argue for focusing military, intelligence, and counterterrorism resources on tightly targeted operations that minimize civilian casualties.[2]

The Leadership Group believes that the U.S. needs to integrate this current thinking about counterinsurgency into a comprehensive framework to meet our security and foreign policy interests more effectively, and to restore U.S. standing and stature in the world. That framework must include more effective responses to Muslims' main concerns about U.S. policy. Building partnerships that better meet those concerns will enable and motivate the vast majority of Muslims to reject extremism, and will enhance the impact of counterinsurgency operations to deter and disrupt violent extremist groups.[3]

---

1   See for example "The Terrorism Index," *Foreign Policy,* September/October 2008.

2   See e.g. U.S. Secretary of Defense Robert Gates, Landon Lecture (Kansas State University), November 26, 2007, available at www.defenselink.mil; Joseph McMillan and Christopher Cavoli, "Countering Global Terrorism," in Stephen Flanagan and James Schear, eds., *Strategic Challenges: America's Global Security Agenda* (Washington, DC: National Defense University Press and Potomac Books, 2008); Kilcullen, "Countering Global Insurgency," op. cit.; and Gompert, Gordon et al., *War by Other Means,* op. cit.

3   It is important to note that changes in U.S. policies will not necessarily lead to changes in anti-U.S. beliefs and attitudes. The U.S. will need a deliberate, strategic communications strategy to overcome strongly held beliefs with compelling evidence and messages of change and partnership. Alan Whittaker, Dean of the Faculty and Academic Programs, Industrial College of the Armed Forces, personal communication, August 2008.

Assessment of the Underlying Problems

Complementary interests, conflicting perceptions. The Leadership Group begins from the premise, strongly supported by the public opinion research summarized earlier, that large majorities of Americans and Muslims around the world are far more united than divided in many of their core interests: peaceful coexistence and constructive relations among nations; the rule of law and good governance; economic opportunities for individuals and nations; and respect for religious faith and its public expression.

Though there are important differences in views on some important social issues, such as the institutional role of religion in shaping law and public policy, or women's rights, it is clear that the underlying problem is not that Muslims "hate Americans for who we are." On a practical level, there are many strong and ongoing partnerships between U.S. public and private institutions and their counterparts in Muslim countries. These partnerships are supporting political reform and economic development, helping to manage and resolve conflicts, and promoting people-to-people exchange and dialogue.

There are, however, significant differences in how most Americans and most Muslims perceive each other's intentions and actions on specific issues. Broadly, many Americans believe that the U.S. government is seeking to maintain positive relations with Muslim countries and peoples, and is acting legitimately in self-defense in its responses to hostile governments and extremist groups. Many Muslims take a very different view. They perceive the U.S. government to be disrespectful of Muslim values, indifferent to Muslim interests, and interested in controlling Muslim countries and regions. Some perceive the U.S. as antagonistic to their religion.

When considering Muslim intentions and actions, Americans are often uncertain how to gauge the breadth and depth of support for extremist groups and hostile governments across the Muslim world. As noted earlier, large majorities of Muslims are highly critical of the 9/11 attacks and of all attacks on civilians, but many share extremists' judgment that there is a legitimate right of self-defense against what they see as unjust and harmful actions by the U.S. and its allies.

The Leadership Group recognizes both the important complementary interests and the strong differences in perceptions on specific issues. In order to make progress in improving relations, the Leadership Group seeks to identify the core causes of tension, and to frame responses that take account of both the U.S. national interests at stake and the concerns of Muslims around the world.

Core causes of tension. In the Leadership Group's view, public opinion data and the actions of Muslim and U.S. leaders suggest five drivers of tension between people across the Muslim world and the U.S.:

- *Violent conflicts in Israel, Palestine, Iraq, Afghanistan, and Pakistan, and heightened tensions with Iran.* For hundreds of millions of Muslims around the world, the Israeli-Palestinian conflict and the conflict in Iraq have become symbols of oppression and occupation of Muslim people and territory. The U.S. confrontation with Iran has added to the widespread perception that the U.S. intends to dominate the Middle East militarily for the foreseeable future.[4] Recent changes in U.S. policy and action have begun to address these concerns, but there is an urgent need to strengthen and sustain the shifts that the U.S. has begun to make.

- *Muslim extremist attacks on civilians in the U.S., Europe, and Muslim-majority countries.* For most Americans, the 9/11 attacks and their perpetrators are a primary driver of tensions. Many Americans are also aware of the bombings in Bali, Madrid, and London that killed hundreds of Western civilians, and of attacks in Iraq, Afghanistan, Pakistan, Saudi Arabia, Turkey, and Morocco that have killed thousands of Muslim civilians. These attacks have fueled U.S. fears of Muslim extremism, questions about its cultural and religious drivers, and a determination to strike back in order to prevent future attacks.

---

4   Not all Muslims in the Middle East oppose the U.S. in its confrontation with Iran. Leaders in a number of Sunni majority countries favor U.S.-led containment of Iran.

- *U.S. relationships with authoritarian governments.* To maintain near-term political stability and security of oil supplies, and promote cooperation in countering extremist groups, the U.S. has supported authoritarian governments. Yet these relationships have arguably undermined long-term U.S. and Muslim interests and values favoring the rule of law, respect for human rights, representative government, diversified economies, and sustainable energy policies. Though the U.S. has recently begun to advocate democratic reform in some Muslim countries, many Muslims question the U.S. commitment, seeing mixed signals in U.S. policy and practice.

- *Serious limitations on economic opportunity in many Muslim countries and Muslim minority communities, which contribute to a widespread sense of frustration, especially among young people.* Though the U.S. is not directly responsible for the economic problems of Muslim countries, its close alliances with authoritarian governments make it a convenient scapegoat for extremists who argue that the U.S. uses corrupt governments to maintain control of oil, fund military budgets, and channel aid to its client states.

- *Serious misunderstanding, distrust, and disrespect between non-Muslim Americans and Muslim communities.* Pervasive, societal mistrust is an issue in its own right and a consequence of the tensions listed here. The current gap in perceptions and beliefs about each other's motives and values seriously constrains the ability of U.S. and Muslim leaders to improve relations.

We recognize that deliberately inflammatory statements by some Muslim leaders, and inaccurate political commentary in the press in many Muslim countries, have contributed to the climate of mistrust, misunderstanding, and disrespect. Nonetheless, if improving relations with Muslim countries is a major foreign policy goal of the U.S., these tensions must be addressed in ways that take account of Muslim perceptions.

Proposing a New Strategy

The Leadership Group recommends a new strategy to substantially improve U.S. relations with Muslim countries and communities within the next several years. The strategy has four goals. Together, they are the pillars on which the U.S. can build strong and mutually beneficial relationships with Muslim counterparts:

- *Pillar 1: Elevate diplomacy as the primary tool for resolving key conflicts involving Muslim countries, engaging both allies and adversaries in dialogue*

- *Pillar 2: Support efforts to improve governance and promote civic participation in Muslim countries, and advocate for principles rather than parties in their internal political contests*

- *Pillar 3: Help catalyze job-creating growth in Muslim countries to benefit both the U.S. and Muslim countries' economies*

- *Pillar 4: Improve mutual respect and understanding between Americans and Muslims around the world*

The need for more collaborative, multilateral approaches is a theme that cross-cuts all four pillars.

Efforts on any one of the pillars will be helpful, but coordinated action on all four pillars offers the greatest potential for improvements in U.S. security and U.S.-Muslim relations. For example, conflict resolution requires a base of mutual respect and understanding, and progress in conflict resolution can contribute to greater mutual respect and understanding over time. Conflict resolution can also create openings for improved governance and economic reform, by enabling a shift of public attention to domestic issues. More effective governance is a prerequisite for economic growth, and job-creating growth can contribute to better governance and greater civic participation.

For acute conflict countries that are also fragile states—Iraq,

Afghanistan, and Palestine, among others—simultaneous and coordinated action on all four pillars is a necessity. To gain the most from the strategy in other countries and regions, U.S. leaders and their counterparts have to determine when to act sequentially on the pillars and when to work in parallel. Finally, at the global level, the U.S. can do a great deal to improve international cooperation on all four pillars by working through the United Nations and other multilateral institutions, through public diplomacy, and through public-private partnerships.

In the following sections, we explain why action on each pillar is essential for improving U.S.-Muslim relations, and provide more detail on the specific actions needed to make progress.

Elevate diplomacy as the primary tool for resolving key conflicts involving Muslim countries, engaging both allies and adversaries in dialogue   1

- *Engage with Iran to explore the potential for agreements that could increase regional security, while seeking Iran's full compliance with its nuclear nonproliferation commitments*

- *Work intensively for immediate de-escalation of the Israeli-Palestinian conflict and a viable path to a two-state solution, while ensuring the security of Israelis and Palestinians*

- *Promote broad-based political reconciliation in Iraq, and clarify the long-term U.S. role*

- *Renew international commitment and cooperation to halt extremists' resurgence in Afghanistan and Pakistan*

- *Provide top-level U.S. leadership to resolve regional conflicts and to improve coordination with international partners*

Majorities of Muslims around the world are intensely concerned with what they perceive as a U.S. effort to dominate Muslim countries in the Middle East and Asia. They see U.S. involvement in the Israeli-Palestinian conflict as favoring Israel; the U.S. occupation of Iraq as self-serving aggression; the U.S. confrontation with Iran as an attempt to overthrow the only Muslim government that has demonstrated an ability to check U.S. ambitions in the region; the U.S. and North Atlantic Treaty Organization (NATO) presence in Afghanistan as a counterterrorism and counterinsurgency campaign that has failed to promote economic and political development for the Afghan people; and Pakistan as a client state whose rulers are dependent on the U.S.

There is both complementarity and contrast in U.S. public views of these conflicts. Most Americans believe the U.S. should be a balanced and fair mediator in the Israeli-Palestinian conflict, though historically majorities have sympathized with Israel. Most want the U.S. to withdraw from Iraq as soon as a stable government acceptable to the country's main ethnic and sectarian groups can be created. Most favor a diplomatic resolution of the tensions with Iran. And most believe that defeating the Taliban is necessary as a basis for political and economic development in Afghanistan.[5]

It may not be possible to bridge fully the gap in perceptions about the U.S. role in this set of conflicts. It may be possible, however, to manage the four major conflicts in ways that advance U.S. interests and also address the core concerns of Muslims within the region and around the world.

The Bush administration has recently begun dialogue with Iran on security issues in Iraq and on Iran's nuclear program, sought to revive the Israeli-Palestinian peace process, increased its focus on the political issues in the Iraqi conflict, gained additional NATO commitments to

---

5   U.S. public opinion on the Israeli-Palestinian conflict is surveyed in Robert Ruby, "Six-Day War: Its Aftermath in American Public Opinion," Pew Forum on Religion & Public Life, May 30, 2007, available at www.pewforum.org. See also PIPA, "International Poll: Most Publics—including Americans—Oppose Taking Sides in Israeli-Palestinian Conflict," July 1, 2008. U.S. public opinion on Iraq, Iran, and the Taliban is surveyed in Public Agenda and *Foreign Affairs*, "Confidence in U.S. Foreign Policy Index," Spring 2008, op. cit.

help stabilize Afghanistan, and committed to work with the new civilian government of Pakistan. It is essential that the next Administration strengthen and build on these initiatives, with a "diplomatic surge" that is highly visible and carefully managed to achieve substantial results in the Administration's first 18 months.

Engage with Iran to explore the potential for agreements that could increase regional security, while seeking Iran's full compliance with its nuclear nonproliferation commitments. Because of Iran's strategic position between Iraq and Afghanistan, the size of its population and economy, its military power, and its regional political actions and ambitions, it is arguably the single most influential Muslim country with which the U.S. is in conflict.

Since the fall of the Shah in 1979, the U.S. has had no formal diplomatic relations with Iran, and has treated Iran primarily as an adversary to be contained. Today, Iran's influence is significantly greater because the U.S. has removed two hostile regimes on its borders: Saddam Hussein's Iraq to the west and the Taliban's Afghanistan to the east.

Iran has taken advantage of the fall of these regimes to expand its influence dramatically in Iraq. It has also increased its influence in Lebanon and Palestine through its ongoing support for Hezbollah and Hamas and their military operations. In parallel, Iran has pursued a nuclear enrichment program in a manner that has raised serious questions about its interest in nuclear weapons and its capacity to develop them. Iran has also, however, provided support to create the new government in Afghanistan, and did offer the U.S. support and cooperation in the effort to capture or kill al-Qaeda members in the early stages of the Afghanistan war.

Currently, the U.S. and Iran have several sharp conflicts of interest. The U.S. seeks limits to Iran's nuclear program, and an end to Iranian support for militias in Iraq, the military operations of Hezbollah in Lebanon, and the military operations of Hamas in Palestine. Iran seeks an end to U.S.-supported international diplomatic and economic sanctions, threats of U.S. military intervention, and support for groups that seek to overthrow Iran's government.

Yet the U.S. and Iran may also have a number of important shared interests: limiting the influence and operational capacity of extremist Sunni groups in Iraq and Afghanistan; avoiding nuclear proliferation in the Middle East; and ensuring respect for the rights of Shiite populations in predominantly Sunni countries.

Given this complex mix of competing and complementary interests, the U.S. needs to change its strategy with Iran. The U.S. has done a great deal to signal to Iran that it is prepared to use force if absolutely necessary to protect core U.S. interests in the region. This approach has not succeeded in limiting Iran's influence in the region, or in undermining those in Iran's government who have been most hostile to the U.S. In the foreseeable future, it is very unlikely that the U.S. can isolate Iran from its allies in the region. It is also unlikely that the U.S. and its allies (both Muslim and Western) could do substantially more to constrain Iran's economic or military options, or undermine its government, without resorting to force.[6]

At this point, the U.S. should expand the contacts with Iran that the Bush administration has recently initiated.[7] The goal of an expanded dialogue should be to explore the potential for mutually beneficial agreements on regional security, diplomatic and economic relations. At the same time, the U.S. should continue seeking international verification of Iran's compliance with its commitments under the Nuclear Non-Proliferation Treaty.[8]

---

6 On the problems of the containment strategy, see Vali Nasr and Ray Takeyh, "The Costs of Containing Iran," *Foreign Affairs,* January/February 2008.

7 The Bush Administration has held several bilateral meetings with Iran on security issues in Iraq. In July 2008, the Administration sent a high-level envoy to participate in ongoing talks with Iran on the nuclear issue. The State Department has also stated that it is considering opening an interests section in Iran. See e.g. Stephen Lee Myers, "U.S. Envoy to Join Meeting with Iranian," *New York Times,* July 16, 2008.

8 If necessary, the U.S. should seek agreement through the UN Security Council, and specifically with Britain, France, Germany, Russia, China, and India, on additional sanctions to be implemented if international inspectors cannot regularly and systematically verify Iran's compliance with its nonproliferation commitments. See for example Anatol Lieven and Trita Parsi's proposal for the U.S. to push for an international agreement to "place a verifiable cap on Iranian enrichment and other nuclear capabilities well short of weaponization ... a red line that all states of the UN Security Council agree on, and which Iran itself has always said that it accepts." "Drawing a Red Line with Iran," *International Herald Tribune,* July 28, 2008.

Members of the Leadership Group have a range of views on Iran's intentions, and on the likelihood that direct discussions between the U.S. and Iran will prove productive. It may not be possible to alter Iran's behavior through dialogue, and there should be no illusions about the regional and international danger if Iran were to weaponize its nuclear program. Nonetheless, the Leadership Group's members agree on two key points. First, opening direct dialogue does not mean meeting any of Iran's current demands, or putting long-standing alliances with Israel, Saudi Arabia, or other states in the region at risk. Second, a carefully prepared dialogue with authoritative Iranian leaders should be tried to see if it is possible to reach a phased series of agreements that could significantly reduce tensions across the region.[9]

If dialogue on the core issues of concern—the nuclear program, security guarantees, and Iraq—goes well, the U.S. and Iran could broaden it to address wider regional security issues. The long-range goal should be a new regional security agreement, with the U.S., Iran, Saudi Arabia, Israel, Syria and other regional powers committing themselves to nonaggression, regional arms control, and creation of a standing mechanism for addressing security concerns.[10] Though a regional security framework seems hard to imagine today, naming it as a real possibility could provide stronger incentives for the U.S., Iran, and other countries to work for resolution of their current conflicts. In any case, seeing whether a serious dialogue is possible should be part of any strategy to dissuade Iran from pursuing nuclear weapons.

Work intensively for immediate de-escalation of the Israeli-Palestinian conflict and a viable path to a two-state solution. U.S. leadership in resolving the Israeli-Palestinian conflict is critical not only for Israelis

---

9   For further analysis of major issues and the potential for mutually beneficial agreements, see William Luers, Thomas R. Pickering and Jim Walsh, "A Solution for the U.S.-Iran Nuclear Stand-off," *The New York Review of Books* 55, no. 4 (March 20, 2008).

10 Regional arms control could focus on reducing conventional forces, and could also seek to achieve a Middle East verifiably free of nuclear weapons and other weapons of mass destruction, in the context of comprehensive regional peace agreements. For current U.S. policy on this issue, see U.S. Department of State, "Nonproliferation and the Middle East," April 19, 2007, available at www.state.gov.

and Palestinians, but also for U.S. relations with Muslim countries and people world-wide. It would be hard to overstate the symbolic significance of the conflict, and the U.S. role in it, for Muslims in the Middle East and around the world. In the view of most Muslims, the U.S. has enabled and shielded Israel's occupation of Palestinian lands since 1967. When they consider the record of U.S. support for Israel, and the U.S. decision to deny the legitimacy of Hamas following its 2006 electoral victory, they find it easy to reject U.S. calls for democracy in other Muslim countries.[11]

Helping to de-escalate the Israeli-Palestinian conflict and put it on a sustainable path to a two-state solution would contribute greatly to U.S. credibility across the Muslim world. Middle East states that have exploited the conflict to distract attention from their domestic failings might also face greater pressure to accelerate political and economic reforms.

Israelis, Palestinians, the U.S., and other key players in the region and around the world recognize that the status quo is untenable. Israel's occupation of the West Bank and its isolation of Gaza, the status of Jerusalem, and Palestinian terrorist attacks in Israel undermine security for all, encouraging extremism and making it nearly impossible for leaders on either side to create a comprehensive peace agreement.

Today, the critical question is not whether to sacrifice Israel's security for the sake of Muslim public opinion, or vice versa. Rather, it is what practical steps the U.S. can take to help Palestinians achieve their rights to security and self-determination, while maintaining and enhancing Israel's security.

The Bush administration began trying to reverse the polarization with a November 2007 conference at Annapolis and has made substantial efforts to build momentum in subsequent peace talks. However, there are serious difficulties with the design of the Annapolis process. Most serious is that the initial commitments the U.S. has asked both the Palestinian Authority and the Israeli government to fulfill, based

---

11   Whether or not one agrees with these perceptions, they are undoubtedly widespread. See e.g. Shibley Telhami, "Does the Palestinian-Israeli Conflict Still Matter?" Saban Center for Middle East Policy, Analysis Paper No. 17, June 2008 (Washington, DC: Brookings Institution, 2008).

on the 2003 "Roadmap" (for example, reform and unification of Palestinian security forces and removal of Israeli checkpoints in the West Bank), may be politically unattainable in the short-term. By pushing hard on a set of requirements that probably cannot be met, the U.S. risks undermining the credibility of leaders on both sides, and ultimately risks rejection of the Annapolis initiative as a whole.

To increase the chances of success, the U.S. needs to help Israeli and Palestinian leaders by refocusing the negotiation process on a set of goals that are achievable in the next year. Specifically:

- Halting Israeli settlement construction in the Palestinian Territories, based on an unambiguous and jointly agreed definition of "new settlement construction"

- Prosecuting Palestinian extremists who incite violence in the West Bank (where Palestinian President Abbas can make and follow through on commitments)

- Rebuilding security cooperation by sharing intelligence about planned attacks, taking joint action to prevent them, and cooperating in tracking down and arresting attackers; training Palestinian security forces; and improving treatment of Palestinians at Israeli checkpoints

- Reducing the Israeli military presence (including checkpoints) as the security situation improves and renewing economic exchange between the West Bank and Israel

- Investing in West Bank areas that have benefited from enhanced security, focusing on education, and on social and municipal services that directly contribute to the quality of life on a daily basis

The U.S. has a critical role to play in defining the benchmarks for performance of these commitments, monitoring their implementation, and fostering accountability for fulfilling them. Only with meaningful, substantial progress toward these initial goals can the parties begin serious discussions on final status issues.

As negotiations move forward, the U.S. should also coordinate diplomacy closely with other key international and regional actors, including the other members of the Quartet, the Arab League, the Organization of the Islamic Conference, and the governments of Saudi Arabia, Egypt, Jordan, Turkey, and potentially Iran. Together with the U.S., these actors can strengthen incentives for both Israelis and Palestinians to move toward a permanent resolution.

The role of Hamas and its control of Gaza remain a serious challenge to the U.S. and other Quartet members, Israel, the Palestinian Authority, and Arab states who seek a mutually acceptable resolution of the conflict. The strongest source of U.S. leverage with Hamas may be a U.S. dialogue with Iran, discussed earlier, that could lead to a reduction in Iranian support for Hamas' military operations.

In addition or as an alternative, the U.S. should use indirect channels (through Egypt, Saudi Arabia, and potentially Syria) to assess the potential usefulness of engaging Hamas in dialogue to try to affect its behavior. Exploratory discussions should make it clear that the U.S. will respond constructively to Hamas only if Hamas changes its policies and behavior toward Israel and the Palestinian Authority. A sustained Hamas ceasefire with Israel, and a mutually acceptable resolution of political representation questions with the Palestinian Authority, should be the basis for any substantial change in the U.S. stance toward Hamas. Direct engagement with Hamas should take place only after Hamas acceptance of the Quartet conditions, and should be coordinated with Israel and the Palestinian Authority.[12]

To build momentum for a broader regional peace, the U.S. should also engage Syria in dialogue. Moderates in Israel, Palestine, and Lebanon could all gain if dialogue led to a realignment of Syrian foreign policy toward peace with Israel and full self-determination in Lebanon. As a

---

12 The Quartet Statement of January 30, 2006, S031/06, indicates that "all members of a future Palestinian government must be committed to nonviolence, recognition of Israel, and acceptance of previous agreements and obligations, including the Roadmap."

core element of dialogue and diplomacy with Syria, the U.S. should help mediate and guarantee a Syrian-Israeli peace treaty, and seek ways to normalize Damascus-Washington relations, while encouraging the on-going restoration of diplomatic relations between Syria and Lebanon.

To knit these threads together, the U.S. needs a carefully designed, sustained, and energetic strategy. Too often in the past, the U.S. commitment has been episodic. The track record of U.S. diplomacy in the region shows the high risk that misunderstanding, mistrust, and the actions of hard-liners and extremists pose to the peace process. On the other hand, high-level and sustained U.S. efforts have helped the parties to achieve substantial agreements, and could do so again.

As the leader of sustained U.S. efforts to achieve a permanent, two-state resolution of the Israeli-Palestinian conflict, the President should appoint a Special Envoy. The Envoy should have stature, credibility, and authority comparable to that of Senator George Mitchell in the Northern Ireland peace process. Specifically, the Special Envoy should have the authority to publicly state, monitor, and report on the commitments of the parties, and their actions to meet those commitments. He or she should have direct access to the President and the authority to speak for the President when appropriate. The success or failure of U.S. efforts will depend heavily on the skills and credibility of the Special Envoy. The President and Secretary of State should aim to make the appointment within the first three months of the Administration.

Promote broad-based political reconciliation in Iraq, and clarify the long-term U.S. role. In Iraq, the "surge" in U.S. forces has helped Baghdad and other areas of the country move toward greater stability. The national government has made some steps toward national reconciliation through a law providing political openings to former Baathists, and a commitment to provincial elections. Nonetheless, the security gains are fragile, and can only be sustained if there is a national political resolution of several outstanding issues. The key political issues include the division of powers among national, regional, and provincial governments; the distribution of oil revenues; command and control of government security forces; and the integration or disbanding of militias. The U.S. needs to build on the local and provincial agreements it has reached with Sunnis to combat al-Qaeda-linked extremists, and to create a more comprehensive set of agreements among Sunni, Shiite, and Kurdish leaders on the major issues.

To do so, the U.S. needs to broaden the set of actors involved in political reconciliation, including political and civic leaders currently outside the Iraqi Parliament. The UN's renewed Assistance Mission for Iraq (UNAMI) may be a significant ally in the reconciliation process, building on its work in organizing provincial elections. The U.S. and the Iraqi government should also seek more active involvement of the UN, the World Bank, and other multilateral, bilateral, and nongovernmental agencies (NGOs) in civilian "nation building" operations (for example, reforming the justice and electoral systems, strengthening the planning and management capacity of provincial and local government, building health and education systems, and promoting community-level reconciliation). In many of these areas the U.S. has limited capacities; expanding the number of partners involved could enhance the legitimacy as well as the effectiveness of reconstruction efforts.[13]

Iraq's neighbors have important roles to play as well. Iran is a critically important influence on a number of Shiite political leaders. Saudi Arabia and Jordan have significant influence with some Sunni political and insurgent groups. And Turkey has strong concerns about the cross-border impact of Iraq's autonomous Kurdish area on its Kurdish population. The U.S. and the Iraqi government need to reach agreements with Iran, Saudi Arabia, Jordan, and Turkey, to address their concerns and de-escalate their involvement in the conflict.

The next Administration has an opportunity to create a multilateral partnership to support Iraq's economic and political development. It is essential to ensure that the military, financial, and political resources committed to Iraq are sufficient to prevent a slide into anarchy, while moving as quickly as possible toward full Iraqi self-government.

---

13 For a detailed assessment of ways in which international partners can complement U.S. civil efforts, see. Gompert, Gordon et al., *War by Other Means,* op. cit., esp. Ch. 11, "Multilateral COIN."

For the national and regional reconciliation process to succeed in the long run, the U.S. needs to provide greater clarity about our long-term intentions in Iraq. The Iraqi government needs long-term security, and economic and political assistance to achieve and maintain stability, whatever the next Administration decides about levels of U.S. forces. Yet the Iraqi and U.S. debates on U.S. military deployment show that both U.S. and Iraqi leaders and publics are divided on the future U.S. military commitment to Iraq.[14] American political and military leaders, including President Bush, have stated that the U.S. has no intention of establishing permanent bases.[15] Ongoing negotiations between the U.S. and Iraq have made substantial progress on a framework for drawing down U.S. forces, contingent on the security situation in Iraq.[16] However, the U.S. Presidential candidates have debated the pace at which troops can be drawn down and the length of time that U.S. should expect to maintain troops in Iraq.

In the Leadership Group's view, there are several factors that should drive U.S. decisions on troop levels: the Iraqi government's sovereign decisions on the future U.S. military presence, taking into account the government's ability to provide security; the legitimacy and impartiality of U.S. deployments and operations in the eyes of U.S. and Iraqi leaders and the public; and most importantly, the relationship between the U.S. military presence and the resolution of the outstanding political issues in Iraq. The test should be whether the U.S. can provide security in ways that contribute to the construction of a stable, representative political system in Iraq; with the support of a cross-sectarian majority of the Iraqi people; at a cost that is acceptable to the American public; and with an ongoing, substantial transfer of responsibility to Iraqi security forces.

---

14 See Greg Bruno, "U.S. Security Arrangements and Iraq," Council on Foreign Relations, June 6, 2008, available at www.cfr.org.

15 E.g. President Bush on "FOX News Sunday," February 11, 2008, transcript available at www.foxnews.com, and U.S. Ambassador to Iraq Ryan Crocker's remarks of June 5, 2008, available at iraq.usembassy.gov.

16 See Stephen Farrell, "Draft Accord With Iraq Sets Goal of 2011 Pullout," *New York Times,* August 21, 2008.

Renew international commitment and cooperation to halt extremists' resurgence in Afghanistan and Pakistan. The conflict in Afghanistan does not have the same level of symbolic significance for most Muslims as the conflicts in the Middle East, and the American public has paid less attention to Afghanistan than to Iraq. However, Afghanistan has very high strategic significance as a base for al-Qaeda and the Taliban, and as a test of the ability of an international coalition to translate counterinsurgency into long-term security, economic and political development.

Today, the political, military, and economic situation in Afghanistan is deteriorating. The government does not have the capacity to maintain order or provide basic services across the country, and the NATO-led International Security Assistance Force has not been able to contain the spread of Taliban influence in the south and east of the country. Opium production now dominates the economy, but there is disagreement among international actors and Afghanistan's government on how to attack the opium trade and provide alternative livelihoods.

It is essential to U.S. national security and to the future of the Afghan people that the Taliban gain no further ground. It is also essential that the key foreign governments and multilateral actors (the U.S., Pakistan, Britain, Canada, Germany, NATO, the UN, and the EU), work more collaboratively with each other and the Afghan government to deal with the insurgency, build the government's capacity and accountability, and invest in basic infrastructure. The U.S. has a particularly important role to play in working with Pakistan's government and military to limit the Taliban's ability to operate from Pakistani territory. At the same time, the U.S. must address Pakistan's interest in negotiating with the Taliban to resolve conflicts in tribal areas on the Pakistan-Afghanistan border (discussed later). The U.S. also has a strong interest in finding out whether Iran can play a more constructive role in stabilizing Afghanistan (as discussed earlier).

Provide top-level U.S. leadership to resolve regional conflicts and to improve coordination with international partners. To drive and coordinate regional diplomacy and signal the seriousness of the U.S. commitment, the Leadership Group recommends that the next President and

Secretary of State provide consistent, sustained leadership at the highest levels, and empower senior U.S. officials to explore potential bilateral and regional security agreements with all governments in the region.

U.S. diplomacy to resolve regional conflicts needs to be coordinated with key regional and global partners. For engaging Iran, key partners include the UN Security Council, European allies, China, Russia, India and Japan; for the Israeli-Palestinian peace process, the Quartet, the Arab League, and the Organization of the Islamic Conference; for Iraq, the UN Security Council and Iraq's neighbors; and for Afghanistan, the UN, NATO, and the EU, as well as Pakistan.

While these conflicts are not inextricably linked, progress on one conflict can affect the potential for progress on others, and the climate for U.S. relations with Muslim countries more generally. Dialogue and negotiation with Iran are particularly important given Iran's direct involvement in both Iraq and the Israeli-Palestinian conflict, and its potential to assist in Afghanistan. It may nevertheless be possible to make progress on both the Iraq and the Israeli-Palestinian conflicts even if dialogue with Iran does not produce agreement. To maximize the chances for success in resolving any one of these conflicts, the next Administration needs to pursue strong diplomatic efforts on all of them without delay.

Support efforts to improve governance and promote civic participation in Muslim countries, and advocate for principles rather than parties in their internal political contests

2

- *Build the capacity of government institutions to deliver services, and of citizens to participate in governance*

- *Advocate consistently for nonviolence, pluralism, and fairness in political contests*

- *Use U.S. leverage with authoritarian governments to promote reforms in governance*

- *Assess the value of engagement with political representatives of armed and activist movements case-by-case, based on their principles, behavior, and level of public support*

- *Support political transitions and the consolidation of reforms in countries at critical "turning points"*

Recent years have seen substantial reforms in a number of Muslim majority countries in the Middle East, North Africa, and Central and South Asia. Nonetheless, a sizable proportion of Muslim countries still have low rankings on civil and political liberties, the effectiveness and perceived legitimacy of government, and other governance indicators.[17] Though the U.S. is not directly responsible for the poor governance that plagues many Muslim countries, it does provide military and economic aid to a number of authoritarian governments that supply oil, cooperate in counterterrorism operations, host U.S. military deployments, or have peace agreements with Israel. Over time, the close relationships between the U.S. government and unpopular rulers have created deep and passionate resentment of the U.S., and have fueled extremists who argue that only the establishment of Islamic theocracies can bring justice.[18]

---

17 It is important to stress the diversity of Muslim country governance institutions and their performance. There is little evidence that the religion of Islam is a strong predictor of governance challenges. Rather, a wide range of economic, historical, and geopolitical factors affects governance and leads to diverse outcomes. See for example Arthur A. Goldsmith, "Muslim Exceptionalism? Measuring the 'Democracy Gap,'" *Middle East Policy,* Fall 2007; Saliba Sarsar and David B. Strohmetz, "The Economics of Democracy in Muslim Countries," *Middle East Quarterly,* Summer 2008; and United Nations Development Programme (UNDP), Arab Fund for Economic and Social Development, and Arab Gulf Programme for United Nations Development Organizations, *Arab Human Development Report 2004: Towards Freedom in the Arab World* (Palo Alto: Stanford University Press, 2005).

18 A recent RAND report argues for focusing primarily on improving governance in Muslim states to reduce the base of support for Muslim extremism. It notes, "The greatest weakness in the struggle with Islamic insurgency is not U.S. firepower but the ineptitude and illegitimacy of

Most Americans are skeptical of U.S. efforts to create democracies modeled closely on U.S. institutions, and strongly oppose the use of military force to promote democracy. On the other hand, they do want the U.S. to help reformers who ask for our assistance, and they want the U.S. to support citizens in choosing their leaders through nonviolent politics. They are not deeply concerned about "Islamist" parties coming to power, as long as those parties do not advocate violence and do respect basic human rights. Most Americans, like most Muslims, do not want to see violent extremist movements win power.[19]

Build the capacity of government institutions to deliver services, and of citizens to participate in governance. Elections and other contests for political power in Muslim countries are a major focus of attention for U.S. policy makers, the media, and the public. Less noticed but arguably even more significant in the lives of most citizens is the daily responsiveness and effectiveness of government. Competent, independent judiciaries; executive agencies with transparent policies and operations, and mechanisms for voice and grievance; and legislatures with the capacity to serve as a check on executive institutions—these are critically important for day-to-day accountability and effectiveness in governance. Together, they are the foundation for effective democratic institutions and practices.

The U.S. should increase its support for institutions and organizations that can strengthen the rule of law, civic participation, civil liberties, and government accountability. In some cases, U.S. agencies and quasi-governmental organizations (such as the United States Agency for International Development (USAID) and the National Endowment for Democracy) can be effective funders and program designers; in others, they may choose not to participate, in order to preserve the independence of local institution-building efforts. Similarly, there are

---

the very regimes that are meant to be the alternative to religious tyranny—the ones tagged and targeted as Western puppets by jihad. Success thus hinges on improving the performance and accountability of governments in the Muslim world." See Gompert, Gordon et al., *War by Other Means,* op. cit., p. xxiv.

19　See PIPA, "US Role in the World: Promoting Democracy and Human Rights," 2007.

many countries in which U.S. philanthropies, NGOs, and professional organizations (such as those for judges, lawyers, journalists, and social and environmental advocates) can play a positive role in supporting Muslim counterparts; there are other countries in which it would not be helpful for U.S. organizations to play a visible role.

Where a lead role for the U.S. government and civil society is not useful, the U.S. should support other actors with the legitimacy and capacity to help. The United Nations is the leading global organization with the legitimacy and mandate to work on human rights, governance, and rule of law issues.[20] Many other democratic governments and international NGOs have effective governance and human rights cooperation programs. The U.S. can work in partnership with them, without highlighting its own role, and without tying its fate to specific political actors.

Finally, it is important for the U.S. to recognize the potential for Islamic principles of governance and their advocates to support accountable governance and the rule of law. In many Muslim countries, the most powerful source of legitimacy for reformers today is the Islamic injunction for leaders to rule justly and to be accountable to their people. The U.S. should not equate reform with secularism, nor should it assume that reformers who advocate some form of *Sharia* as the basis for the rule of law will inevitably abuse human rights or adopt anti-American policies.[21]

Advocate consistently for nonviolence, pluralism and fairness in political contests. The current Administration has taken a significant step forward by advocating for political reforms in a number of Muslim countries with authoritarian governments. However, when political openings have allowed militant movements (most notably Hamas in the Palestinian Authority and Hezbollah in Lebanon) to gain popular

---

20   The UN Office of the High Commissioner for Human Rights, UNDP, and other agencies in the UN development system have capacity to assist in particular countries.

21   See for example Noah Feldman, "Why Shariah?" *New York Times Magazine,* March 16, 2008, and Marina Ottaway, "Democracy and Constituencies in the Arab World," Carnegie Paper No. 48, July 2004 (Washington, DC: Carnegie Endowment for International Peace, 2004).

Reapplication of Islamic Principles to Meet the Challenges of the 21st Century

Throughout the Muslim world, reform efforts are underway to reapply the core teachings of Islamic law to meet the emerging challenges of the 21st century. These efforts focus on a variety of issues including consensus building on the interpretation of Islamic law, commitment to nonviolence, and elaboration of Islamic principles of governance. The Amman Message of 2004, the Mecca Declaration of 2006, and most recently the Cordoba Initiative exemplify this trend.

The Amman Message is a religious consensus of Muslim scholars from all major sects, recognizes the legitimacy of different schools of thought within Islam. It rejects the extremist practice of declaring Muslims of other sects or traditions to be apostates, and articulates standards for the issuance of fatwas (religious edicts).

The Mecca Declaration, an initiative of the Organization of the Islamic Conference and the International Islamic Fiqh Academy, categorically forbids sectarian-motivated violence as counter to Islam, while also condemning violence in the name of Islam.

The Cordoba Initiative, an independent, multinational, multifaith project working to improve Muslim-West relations, has recently launched the Sharia Index Project. Its objective is to demystify the notion, meaning, and requirements of an Islamic state, while aiming to clarify and measure how the principles of *Sharia* apply to modern states and their governance.

Learn more about The Amman Message at www.ammanmessage.com, the Mecca Declaration at www.oic-oci.org, and the Cordoba Initiative's Sharia Index Project at www.cordobainitiative.org.

support and win political power through elections, the U.S. has declared them illegitimate, based on their continuing refusal to recognize Israel's right to exist, and their use of violence against Israel and domestic political opponents. The U.S. has also sent mixed signals about its willingness to work with nonviolent Islamist parties, notably the Muslim Brotherhood in Egypt and Jordan. This inconsistency reflects a belief shared among many policy makers that there are significant trade-offs between U.S. security interests and our commitment to political reform. Though understandable, these U.S. responses to militants and nonviolent Islamist parties have confirmed the view of many Muslim citizens and mainstream reformers that the U.S. is not serious about political liberalization in Muslim countries.

In some cases, the strength of U.S. support for political leaders has also been problematic. When the U.S. becomes very closely aligned with one leader or group, it may put longer-term relations with other actors at risk. For example, the U.S. strongly supported General Pervez Musharraf of Pakistan, then shifted its support to Benazir Bhutto as a potential democratic alternative when General Musharraf lost the ability to govern effectively. The closeness of the U.S. embrace actually discredited each leader with important constituencies that distrusted or disagreed with U.S. policies in Pakistan, and made it more difficult for the U.S. to work with other political actors who subsequently came to power.

The U.S. needs to reduce the tension between its stated commitment to reform and its concern about the outcomes of political contests. By advocating for widely shared principles—nonviolence, pluralism, and fair contestation—to govern the competition for power, the U.S. can more legitimately promote political reform without taking sides in internal political contests.

Nonviolence should apply both to authoritarian governments, who should allow nonviolent dissent and political opposition, and to militant political parties, who should use popular mobilization, not militias, to advance their goals.[22] Pluralism should mean that all political groups that are willing to engage in a nonviolent political process

---

22 As one member of the Leadership Group put it, militants should have to choose "ballots or bullets, but not both."

have opportunities to organize, express their views, and compete for popular support.

Fair contestation should mean that the rules for political competition do not bias the outcome in favor of a particular party or faction. Fair contestation does not have to mean one-person, one-vote elections. Negotiations to create power-sharing agreements, for example, can also be governed by rules that ensure all parties have an opportunity to seek a share of power, and agreed criteria for allocating power, without requiring a popular vote.[23]

Use U.S. leverage with authoritarian governments to promote reforms in governance. To be consistent in its advocacy for principles of good governance and accountability, the U.S. cannot accept token gestures of reform by authoritarian governments as the price of continuing U.S. support.[24] By failing to maintain consistency, the U.S. not only fails to make progress, but also loses credibility with reformers and the public. For example, President Mubarak of Egypt did allow parliamentary elections in 2005 and municipal elections this year (after a two year delay), but has continued to suppress opposition leaders and movements. The muted U.S. response to President Mubarak's repeated crackdowns has contributed to the high levels of anti-American hostility in Egypt, despite the fact that Egypt has received more U.S. economic aid than any other Muslim country during the past 30 years.

In order to make its commitment to reform credible, the U.S. needs

---

23 Political power in Lebanon, for example, has been allocated on a confessional basis throughout the country's history, through a mixture of constitutional requirements, elections, and negotiation processes. Though it is a fragile and problematic system, it has restrained the use of violence since the end of the civil war, allowed a measure of pluralism, and provided some measure of fairness in the allocation of power among confessional leaders. Similarly, the 2002 *loya jirga* in Afghanistan aimed to use a nonviolent, plural, and reasonably fair process for selecting a transitional government, without a universal franchise election.

24 Marina Ottaway defines "significant" (as distinct from "cosmetic") reforms as those that "contribute to limiting the power of the executive, allowing the emergence of other centers of power and introducing an element of pluralism." See her chapter "Evaluating Middle East Reform: Significant or Cosmetic?" in Marina Ottaway and Julia Choucair-Vizos, eds., *Beyond the Façade: Political Reform in the Arab World* (Washington, DC: Carnegie Endowment for International Peace, 2008), p. 11.

to calibrate its support for authoritarian governments based on their demonstrated commitment and action to end human rights violations, move toward pluralism, and improve social and economic conditions. The form and extent of U.S. sanctions and incentives can vary based on its relationship with a particular government, and the extent of that government's progress. The U.S. will have to make difficult judgments about providing support in situations where there does not appear to be a viable political force between authoritarian governments and extremist movements seeking to destabilize them and seize power, or where the U.S. has limited leverage with government leaders. Nonetheless, the U.S. should maintain clarity—in its public diplomacy and in its dialogues with governments— about its long-term goal of promoting institutional reforms that favor accountable governance, the rule of law, and public participation.[25]

The governments of Egypt and Saudi Arabia pose particularly difficult challenges for the U.S. Both are close U.S. allies in the search for a peaceful resolution of the Israeli-Palestinian conflict, and in antiterrorism cooperation. However, both countries have consistently poor performance on regional and international measures of good governance.[26]

In Egypt, government repression has contributed to the rise of the Muslim Brotherhood as a major political force. After a period of violent opposition to the Egyptian government, the Brotherhood has moderated some of its goals and strategies as its candidates have been able to participate, tacitly, in parliamentary elections. Other independent Islamist political parties have also begun to organize and compete, but the government continues to limit electoral competition.[27]

Given this context, the primary institutional goal for the U.S. in

---

25 See Council on Foreign Relations, *In Support of Arab Democracy: Why and How? Report of an Independent Task Force* (New York: Council on Foreign Relations, June 2005), for many useful ideas on political reform in the Arab states that can also be applied to other Muslim countries.

26 See for example the assessments of both countries in the UNDP *Arab Human Development Reports* 2002-2005.

27 See Judy Barsalou, "Islamists at the Ballot Box: Findings from Egypt, Jordan, Kuwait and Turkey," United States Institute of Peace (USIP) Special Report No. 144, July 2005 (Washington, DC: USIP, 2005).

Egypt's Civil Society Activists Organize Through Facebook and YouTube

The young Egyptian democracy movement is successfully utilizing Western Internet-based networks to organize beyond the reach of Egypt's secret police. In mid-2007, civil society activist Ahmed Samih, 28, director of the Andalus Institute for Tolerance and Anti-Violence Studies in Cairo, founded a Facebook group titled "What happens when Hosni Mubarak dies?" Six months later, it had grown to 2,741 members and joined some 60 other liberal Egyptian activist groups on Facebook. On YouTube, hundreds of videos range from human rights demonstrations and activist speeches to cell phone footage of torture by the security forces. By opening their networks to activists and resisting government pressure to censor content, U.S. Web sites like Facebook and YouTube are effectively helping local organizations work towards greater political transparency and accountability.

See Jackson Diehl, "Egypt's YouTube Democrats", Washington Post, December 17, 2007.

Egypt should be to create opportunities for political participation and good governance at the local and national level. These opportunities can come not only through elections, but also through increasing the transparency, accountability, and effectiveness of police, municipal services, and the judiciary. The U.S. should also help NGOs and the press to organize to hold local and national government agencies more accountable. Because a substantial majority of Egyptians have negative perceptions of the U.S., it may be most effective for the U.S. to work through multilateral agencies and non-American NGOs to achieve these goals.

In Saudi Arabia, the U.S. has an interest both in domestic political liberalization and in addressing Saudi funding for extremist groups across the Muslim world. Political reform is complicated by internal divisions among members of the royal family; by the domestic balance between the ruling family and the most conservative elements in Saudi society (including, but not limited to, the Wahabi clergy); and by Saudi Arabia's oil wealth, which limits the ability of external actors to influence the royal family's decision making. Addressing funding for extremists is challenging because of the strong commitment of some wealthy and influential Saudis to promote extremist views.[28]

Despite these constraints, King Abdullah has made significant progress in opening up the education system. He has also promoted discussion on reform within the royal family, and has launched an interfaith dialogue effort that is important not only for its implications for interfaith relations, but also for Saudi Arabia's own political and cultural development.[29]

U.S. ability to promote constructive reforms with the Saudi government is limited because we rely on Saudi Arabia to moderate swings in the global supply of oil, and therefore need to protect Saudi Arabia's security and stability in a volatile region. If the U.S. is to increase its ability to promote reform, it will need to reduce its own susceptibility to oil price swings, and seek regional security agreements that reduce Saudi Arabia's vulnerability. These are both long-term endeavors that will require sustained efforts in energy policy and regional diplomacy. However, pursuit of diversified energy supplies and greater regional security will benefit the U.S. in many ways beyond their direct effect on relations with Saudi Arabia.

In the near term, the U.S. has some ability to help promote dialogue and exchange with Saudi Arabia's next generation of leaders through one of our major exports: education. The U.S. is a significant provider of educational opportunities for Saudis, both through Saudi student

---

28 For an overview of the complexity of Saudi Arabia's role, assessing both government efforts to contain extremism and societal support for extremists, see Daniel Byman, "The Changing Nature of State Sponsorship of Terrorism," Saban Center for Middle East Policy, Analysis Paper No. 16, May 2008 (Washington, DC: Brookings Institution, 2008), pp. 19-21. See also Josh Meyer, "Saudis Faulted for Funding Terror," *Los Angeles Times,* April 2, 2008.

29 See Adelle M. Banks, "Saudi King's Conference Rejects Terrorism, Urges Dialogue," Religion News Service, July 18, 2008.

enrollment in U.S. universities and through the establishment of U.S. university programs in Saudi Arabia. Course work and the experience of life in a U.S. university setting can provide Saudi students with a wide range of perspectives on politics, society, and the role of religion in public life. Maintaining and expanding educational opportunities for Saudis in the U.S. and through programs in Saudi Arabia should be a shared goal of U.S. universities and the government. However, education should not be politicized. Rather, the U.S. government's main goals should be to ensure that its visa policy and its treatment of Saudis at the point of entry supports Saudi students' desires to study in the U.S. In addition, it should continue supporting U.S. education programs in Saudi Arabia.

Assess the value of engagement with political representatives of armed and activist movements case-by-case, based on their principles, behavior, and level of public support. The U.S. has difficult choices to make about whether and how to enter into dialogue with movements that have gained political representation through elections, while continuing to use violence against domestic political opponents. Hamas and Hezbollah are arguably in this category. Both are on the U.S. State Department list of terrorist organizations primarily because of their attacks on Israel. Both are also involved in sometimes violent domestic political contests.

There is a range of views within the Leadership Group on the intentions, actions, and legitimacy of Hamas and Hezbollah. There is also a range of views on whether the U.S. should be in dialogue with either or both groups about conditions within their countries, or in regard to the Israeli-Palestinian conflict. Nonetheless, the Group has reached consensus on a set of criteria that the U.S. can use to judge whether, when, and how to engage in dialogue with armed political groups and movements:

- Does the group or movement have a substantial base of legitimate public support, demonstrated by membership, electoral success, and/or mass mobilization? Is this base of support equal to or greater than the apparent support for the current government?

- Does the group have some interests in political, economic, or social reform that are complementary to U.S. interests?

- Have the leaders of the group rejected the use of violence, or shown the willingness and ability to halt the use of violence and give up their arms, when they have had opportunities for nonviolent political competition?

- Is the group a potential spoiler of reform or peace initiatives advocated by mainstream leaders or movements? If so, is the group willing to negotiate participation in a reform coalition or peace process?

- Would U.S. engagement with the group strengthen the position of moderate leaders within the group, relative to those who advocate extremist views and actions?

- If the U.S. needs to explore the preceding questions before engaging publicly in dialogue with the group, does it have informal and/or indirect channels for communicating with the group's leadership, and is there a high likelihood that those communications can remain confidential?[30]

Arguably, the more questions to which the U.S. answer is "yes," the stronger the case for some form of engagement with the armed movement in question.

The U.S. must also consider when and how to talk with political movements that have substantial public support and have renounced violence, but are outlawed or restricted by authoritarian governments

---

30 By "informal" we mean without the formal authorization of the U.S. government; by "indirect" we mean through other governments or political actors, without direct contact between representatives of the U.S. and the movement.

allied to the U.S. The Muslim Brotherhood parties in Egypt and Jordan are arguably in this category. In general, the Leadership Group supports engagement with groups that have clearly demonstrated a commitment to nonviolent participation in politics.[31] However, as noted earlier, the main focus of U.S. engagement should be to help strengthen institutions of governance and civic participation, rather than to support or oppose players in internal political contests.[32]

Support political transitions and the consolidation of reforms in countries at critical "turning points." The U.S. should continually assess prospects for reform in Muslim countries, and should deploy its resources to support reform processes at critical moments without embracing individual reformers or parties too closely. For the most part, reformers who head governments have already demonstrated considerable skill and capacity in mobilizing domestic constituencies, and may not welcome or benefit from highly visible U.S. support. For its part, the U.S. should recognize the risks and uncertainties facing any reformist government, and maintain enough distance to adjust to reversals.

Currently, the government of Pakistan may be well-positioned for reform, and the government of Turkey is at risk of a serious reversal if disputes between secularists and the ruling Justice and Development Party (known by its Turkish acronym AKP) cannot be resolved. Both have critical roles to play in the global effort to build democratic institutions as an alternative to extremism in Muslim countries.

Help restore political balance in Pakistan. Pakistan is a central test case of U.S. commitment to political reform in Muslim countries. Under President Musharraf, Pakistan's government was a strategic ally in

---

31 It is important for the U.S. to assess the rejection of violence not only in practice, but also in principle. The Muslim Brotherhood organizations in Egypt and Jordan have renounced violence against their respective governments but still support the use of violence against Israel by other groups.

32 The U.S. should consider easing visa restrictions on political activists, and allowing more direct contact between U.S. NGOs and activists, in order to promote deeper and more sustained dialogue and relationship building.

the fight against al-Qaeda and the Taliban. At the same time, it defied the international community by continuing clandestine support for extremists in Afghanistan and Kashmir, repressed both moderate and radical political dissent, and increasingly undermined its own constitutional limitations on presidential authority. The 2008 elections and President Musharraf's resignation have dramatically shifted the balance of power to a fragile coalition of political parties aligned with the family of Benazir Bhutto and with former Prime Minister Nawaz Sharif. Also notable is the defeat of extremist parties in the Northwest Frontier Province, signaling that even religiously conservative areas are open to mainstream politics.

Prime Minister Yousaf Raza Gilani has declared a strong interest in using negotiation to resolve the insurgency in the tribal areas bordering Afghanistan. Pakistan's army, the most powerful state institution, is supporting that approach. The government has begun making peace agreements with tribal leaders. However, there is evidence that the reduction in military pressure has allowed militants to mount more numerous and effective attacks on Afghan, U.S., and NATO forces in Afghanistan from inside Pakistan. The current situation raises serious questions about Pakistan's commitment to prevent Taliban forces from operating in Pakistan's border areas.[33]

Despite a shift in policy that has reduced Pakistan's help in the U.S. counterinsurgency and counterterrorism campaigns in the border area, the U.S. has a strong interest in working with the new civilian government as well as Pakistan's military. Historically, the U.S. has had strong relationships with Pakistan's military and with its civilian political leaders, the two institutions that have ruled the country since its independence.

The U.S. needs to renew and strengthen those relationships now, to promote a viable transition from President Musharraf's one-man rule to a more stable civil-military partnership. It is critically important that

---

33 See Jane Perlez, "Pakistan and Taliban Agree to Army's Gradual Pullback," *New York Times*, May 22, 2008; Eric Schmitt, "Militant Gains in Pakistan Said to Draw Fighters," *New York Times*, July 10, 2008; and the August 12, 2008 statement of U.S. National Intelligence Officer Ted Gistaro, op. cit.

the military not step back into politics, that Pakistan's civilian leaders maintain a pluralist political system, and that the new civilian leadership have an opportunity to try a new approach to deal with the tensions in the traditionally autonomous tribal areas. The U.S. should help Pakistan's military and its mainstream political leaders work together to provide incentives for peaceful resolution of the insurgency, while keeping military options open. In the medium term, the U.S. should promote institutional reforms that improve government accountability and service delivery, and broaden the base of political participation in Pakistani society.[34]

Strengthen cooperation with Turkey. Turkey's current government, led by Prime Minister Recep Erdogan and the AKP, is also a key U.S. partner; an example of a nonviolent, mainstream "Islamist" political party governing well in a democracy; an influential actor in the Iraq conflict; and a NATO ally.

While Turkey continues to collaborate with the U.S. on a range of regional security, diplomatic and economic issues, U.S. support for the Kurdish government in northern Iraq has placed some strains on the U.S.-Turkey relationship. Turkey views the Kurdish region of Iraq as a staging ground for Kurdish separatists in southeastern Turkey and Turkey's army has conducted raids on Iraqi territory to attack what it believes to be separatist camps. There are limits to what the U.S. can do to accommodate Turkey's concerns without destabilizing northern Iraq, and there are also legitimate questions for the U.S. to raise about Turkey's treatment of its Kurdish population.[35] Yet even on this issue, there have been positive changes under the AKP: in the summer 2007 elections, a majority of Kurds voted for the national governing party for

---

34　See for example the legislation introduced by Senators Joe Biden and Richard Lugar in July 2008, S. 3263, Enhanced Partnership with Pakistan Act of 2008, to provide substantial additional economic aid to Pakistan over the next ten years, to advance a wide range of governance and development goals. The legislation would make U.S. military aid contingent on ongoing cooperation by Pakistan's military and security services against violent extremists, and would require the military to refrain from involvement in politics.

35　Human Rights Watch, "Turkey: Human Rights Concerns in the Lead up to July Parliamentary Elections," July 2007, available at www.hrw.org.

the first time. Integrating Turkey into a broader regional effort to stabilize Iraq and maintain its territorial integrity, while encouraging the progressive policies of the AKP with regard to Turkey's Kurdish population, is likely to be the best course of action for the U.S. on this issue.

In the medium term, the current Turkish government faces internal challenges from secular conservatives in the military, judiciary, political parties, and civil service, and external challenges from EU members who are resisting Turkey's bid for EU membership. The U.S. has significant influence with Turkey's military, and should encourage Turkey's military to stay out of politics, while respecting the legitimate political contest between secularists and the AKP.

The U.S. has limited ability to affect the EU-Turkey negotiations, and would not help Turkey by taking a strong public stand supporting its membership bid. The U.S. can, however, make the case privately with EU leaders that Turkey is far more likely to be a positive economic and political force in Europe if it is integrated into the EU than if it is excluded. It is especially important that Turkey not be denied membership on grounds that appear to have more to do with its religious and cultural makeup than with its economic or democratic institutions.

3 Help catalyze job-creating growth in Muslim countries to benefit both the U.S. and Muslim countries' economies

- *Support policy reforms to secure property rights, facilitate transactions and promote investments*

- *Partner with governments, multilateral institutions, and philanthropies to make education a more powerful engine of employment and entrepreneurship*

- *Use public-private investment partnerships to reduce risk, promote exports, and fund enterprises*

- *Use trade agreements to reward economic reform and spur investment*

- *Manage energy interdependence and diversify resources*

Poverty and lack of economic opportunity in Muslim majority countries are not the primary cause of anti-U.S. sentiment, nor is the U.S. the primary cause of Muslim countries' economic problems. In the past 20 years, a number of Muslim majority countries (for example, Malaysia and Turkey) have delivered exceptional economic performance. Nevertheless, economic stagnation, the concentration of economic benefits within economic and political elites, and widespread joblessness contribute to a climate of frustration and increase the appeal of extremists in many Muslim countries from North Africa to Southeast Asia.[36]

The U.S. can gain greater security and economic benefits by helping Muslim countries create more productive and competitive economies. One critical goal is to help generate jobs for young people who make up the majority of the population in most Muslim countries and are a growing share of the labor force.

Given the very substantial petrodollar revenues available throughout the Middle East, and the funds available to support large militaries in other countries (for example, Pakistan and Indonesia), the most important economic problem facing many Muslim countries is not the lack of resources for investment. Instead, the core problems in most Muslim countries are limited workforce education and skills, poor infrastructure, political instability, complex and corruption-prone regulations governing finance and commerce, bottlenecks in the flow of information, and weak enforcement of property rights. In turn, these problems deter international investment and weaken many Muslim countries' positions in non-oil trade.[37]

---

36 The Middle East/North Africa region has the highest unemployment rates in the world. See Nimrod Raphaeli, "Unemployment in the Middle East—Causes and Consequences," Inquiry and Analysis Series - No. 265, The Middle East Media Research Institute, February 10, 2006, available at www.memri.org.

37 See for example World Economic Forum, *The Arab World Competitiveness Report 2007*; World

The U.S. public is willing to support initiatives that leverage private sector investment, build the skills and capacities of local entrepreneurs, and promote sustained economic growth. U.S. political support for economic assistance to Muslim countries is likely to be stronger for initiatives that leverage contributions from other countries in the region and from other developed countries, and generate economic benefits for the U.S.[38]

Support policy reforms to secure property rights, facilitate transactions and promote investments. The U.S. government should expand its advocacy and support for policy and regulatory reforms in finance and commerce. Reforms should address the full spectrum of business operations, from registration and operation to contracting and bankruptcy.

To stimulate small and medium enterprise, reforms should make it much easier to register and legally maintain businesses. Reducing barriers to entry will help make businesses more competitive and curtail "informal" economies, which undermine governance, investment, and working conditions in many countries. For business operations, reforms should strengthen not only the legal security of property rights and contracts, but also provide swifter, fairer, and lower-cost enforcement of property and contract laws. In countries that still have criminal penalties for insolvency (bankruptcy), it is imperative to remove those penalties in order to encourage greater risk-taking and remove the stigma from unsuccessful ventures.[39]

U.S. government, academic, and business experts can help Muslim counterparts strengthen laws, courts, and other institutions needed to

---

Bank, *Doing Business 2008: Middle East and North Africa,* 2007; UNDP, *Arab Human Development Report 2005 and 2004;* and Ibrahim Akoum, "It's Better Institutions, Middle East!" Center for International Private Enterprise, Economic Reform Feature Service, May 31, 2006.

38 See PIPA, "US Role in the World," op. cit., and "Americans on Foreign Aid and World Hunger," February 2, 2001.

39 For a detailed presentation of the linkages between legal rights and economic development benefiting low income entrepreneurs and workers, see *Making the Law Work for Everyone,* Report of the Commission on Legal Empowerment of the Poor, Volume I (New York: UNDP and the Commission on Legal Empowerment of the Poor, 2008).

Qatari Government Takes on Corruption

In December 2007, the Emir of Qatar announced the creation of the National Committee for Integrity and Transparency (NCIT) as an attempt to step up the fight against corruption. The NCIT combats corruption on two levels: it seeks to develop legislation and practices to prevent and investigate corruption, and it works to nurture a culture of integrity through the education system. In June 2008, the NCIT hosted a conference entitled "Corruption-Free Asia: A Long-Term Vision" to further these objectives, recognizing that curtailing corruption encourages international investment and economic growth.

See Mohammad Iqbal, "Qatar adopts 5-year strategy to fight graft," The Peninsula, June 11, 2008.

define and enforce business registration, property rights, and contract and insolvency laws.

In addition, the U.S. should support efforts to liberalize banking and create banking services for small and medium enterprises. Banks in the U.S. and other countries are already working in Muslim countries to integrate systems that use Islamic financing principles with Western systems.[40] U.S. assistance will be most effective if it is coordinated with European and Asian governments and channeled through multilateral programs.[41]

The next President could demonstrate U.S. commitment to improving economic opportunities by co-convening a high-level meeting on economic reform and job creation in the Middle East in the next Administration's first year. Co-convening partners could include heads of state from the regions and multilateral institutions (for example,

---

40 Assif Shameen, "Islamic Banks: A Novelty No Longer," *BusinessWeek,* August 8, 2005.

41 The OECD-MENA Investment Programme and the International Finance Corporation Private Enterprise Partnership-MENA are notable ongoing multilateral initiatives to support economic reform and improve the climate for private enterprise in 19 countries in the Middle East and North Africa.

the Organisation for Economic Co-operation and Development and/ or the World Bank). Together, the leaders could reaffirm their commitment to ongoing reforms, and launch one or more new initiatives to promote job creation in the region. If well-prepared, this meeting could make an important contribution to improving both the climate for investment in the Middle East and business opportunities for U.S.-based companies.

Partner with governments, multilateral institutions, and philanthropies to make education a more powerful engine of employment and entrepreneurship. There is broad consensus in the economic development field that education is the foundation for sustained and diversified growth. In many Muslim countries as in other developing countries, there are serious limitations in the coverage and quality of primary and secondary education. Business-oriented education at the secondary and university level is even more limited.[42]

Governments play a critical role in providing public education at all levels, but there is limited accountability for results. In some countries, cultural and religious restrictions on girls' education, and the availability of subsidized religious education that is even less relevant to employment and entrepreneurship, pose additional challenges to public education systems.

Because of the sensitivity of education as a core element of national identity and culture, the U.S. government should focus its efforts on partnering with governments committed to reform, and with multilateral agencies that have credibility and capacity to promote school enrollment, high quality instruction, and employment-oriented skills training. U.S. education experts and institutions can help build up primary, secondary, technical, and professional schools. Multilateral institutions, including the World Bank and several UN development agencies, can play important roles in providing technical advice and funding to support the development of education systems.

---

42 However, demand for business education is growing rapidly. See Alina Dizik, "The Middle East's Fertile Ground," *BusinessWeek*, March 31, 2008.

U.S. philanthropies and the business sector also have important roles to play. Philanthropic leaders can support catalytic pilot projects. Businesses investing in Muslim majority countries can establish job training programs, not only for their current employees but for potential future employees, through partnerships with secondary schools and universities. By investing in education, U.S. and Muslim governments, educational, philanthropic, and business partners can gain credibility

American Foundation Trains Muslim Job Seekers in Exchange for Job Guarantees

The Washington, DC-based Education for Employment Foundation (EFE) partners with local businesses and universities in Gaza, Jordan, Morocco, and Egypt to run vocational, technical, and managerial training programs for unemployed university graduates. A large majority of trainees who complete the program take well paid, career-building jobs (placement rates are 85-100 percent). The Mini-Master's of Business Administration (MBA) Accounting Training Program, launched in March 2006, is the signature program in Gaza. Its business partner, Consolidated Contractors International Company, a global engineering and construction firm, has committed to hiring or placing 120 graduates over three years. The six-month program starts with an intensive course in business English followed by a mini-MBA program designed by University of Maryland's Robert H. Smith School of Business. It features rigorous, real-life business simulations. The course takes place at EFE's local academic partner, the Islamic University of Gaza. Even though graduates of the Gaza program are mostly placed in the United Arab Emirates rather than in Gaza's distressed economy, these skilled workers may eventually return to rebuild their own economy.

See Lisa Takeuchi Cullen, "Gainful Employment", Time, September 20, 2007, and the Education for Employment Foundation Web site at www.efefoundation.org.

and help transform a high-risk youth generation into a broad and deep pool of skilled workers and managers.

Use public-private investment partnerships to reduce risk, promote exports, and fund enterprises. One critical driver of private investment is safety and security. Success in conflict resolution efforts, as outlined earlier, is a prerequisite for major expansion of U.S. and other international investments in conflict-affected Muslim countries. However, companies in different sectors focus on different kinds of risk, and it may be possible to promote the entry of some kinds of foreign investment (for example, mobile phone networks) at an earlier stage in conflict resolution, while others (for example, large-scale manufacturing) may require a longer period of stability before entering.

Where there is adequate security, the U.S. government and private sector should also create ambitious new public-private investment partnerships with counterparts in the Muslim world, targeting emerging sectors with high potential for job and enterprise creation.[43] Opportunities exist in many sectors, though there are important differences in both challenges and opportunities across different types of economies.[44] For example, the Middle East Investment Initiative (MEII), a joint program of the Overseas Private Investment Corporation, the Palestinian Investment Fund and the Aspen Institute, is providing more than $220 million in loan guarantees to Palestinian entrepreneurs to allow them to expand operations with limited collateral requirements.[45] The U.S.

---

43 U.S. visa policy is currently an obstacle to business partnerships with counterparts across the Muslim world. As suggested in the next section, the U.S. should consider increasing consular resources and changing secondary screening protocols for frequent business travelers from Muslim countries, to increase efficiency and ensure respect, without compromising security.

44 The World Bank distinguishes *labor-importing and resource rich* (Bahrain, Kuwait, Oman, Saudi Arabia, United Arab Emirates), *labor-abundant and resource poor* (Egypt, Jordan, Morocco, Tunisia), *labor-abundant and resource rich* (Algeria, Iran, Libya, Syria), and *conflict-affected* (Afghanistan, Iraq, Lebanon, Pakistan, Palestinian Authority, Yemen) economies in the region. See World Bank, Middle East and North Africa Region: 2007 Economic Developments and Prospects (Washington, DC: World Bank, 2007).

45 See Aspen Institute, "The Middle East Investment Initiative (MEII) Launches in Ramallah," July 2007, available at www.aspeninstitute.org. MEII is also developing home mortgage and political risk guarantee programs.

Palestinian Coca-Cola Franchise Provides Local Jobs and Community Support

The Palestinian franchise of The Coca-Cola Company, the National Beverage Company (NBC), is the second largest private employer in the Palestinian Territories and a key source of jobs in a period of economic stagnation. Established in 1998 as an independent, privately held company run by Palestinian businessmen, NBC employs 200 local people in its bottling plant in Ramallah and distribution centers in Gaza, Hebron, and Nablus, and generates hundreds of additional jobs in related industries. On plant tours, school students learn that even in hard times there are economic prospects in Palestine. NBC also engages in national and community projects, such as sponsorship of the Palestinian national soccer team, special *iftar* meals for orphaned children during Ramadan, and the first children's book libraries in West Bank and Gaza hospitals.

See the National Beverage Company Web site at www.nbc-pal.com.

could complement MEII and other private risk insurance and export promotion programs with enterprise funds like those it established to encourage investment in Eastern Europe after the Cold War.[46]

Sovereign wealth funds, controlled by the governments of oil-producing countries and now holding over a trillion dollars in assets, are a major source of potential investment funds within the region. The vast majority of their capital is now invested outside the region, and a sizable percentage is invested in the U.S.[47]

---

46   United States General Accounting Office, *Foreign Assistance: Enterprise Funds' Contributions to Private Sector Development Vary,* GAO/NSIAD-99-221, September 1999.

47   McKinsey Global Institute, *The New Power Brokers: How Oil, Asia, Hedge Funds, and Private Equity Are Shaping Global Capital Markets,* esp. Ch. 2 (McKinsey & Company, October 2007).

The current financial crisis has led some of the largest U.S. investment and commercial banks to seek additional investment from sovereign wealth funds. In the near future, the U.S. financial services industry and government may wish to maintain the flow of sovereign wealth fund investments into the U.S. economy. Nonetheless, the U.S. has a long-term interest in promoting the investment of at least a small portion of sovereign wealth fund portfolios in job-creating growth in the Middle East. World Bank President Robert Zoellick has proposed that sovereign wealth funds invest one percent of their capital in Africa in partnership with the World Bank.[48] The U.S. should propose a parallel World Bank initiative for the Middle East, in partnership with sovereign wealth funds based there, to stimulate job-creating growth. The World Bank and other multilateral and bilateral agencies could assist in identifying projects and building a diversified portfolio of investments into which sovereign wealth funds could invest.

Use trade agreements to reward economic reform and spur investment.
The U.S. should also expand its use of bilateral free trade agreements, and support regional and global trade integration, to reward economic reform and spark job creation in promising sectors.[49] The U.S.-Jordan Free Trade Agreement of 2001 has brought significant economic benefits to Jordan's exporters, and opened a new market for U.S. exports and investors. The U.S. has concluded similar free trade agreements with Bahrain, Morocco and Oman, and has ongoing negotiations with Malaysia and the United Arab Emirates.[50] The security and geopolitical benefits of using trade to improve U.S.-Muslim relations should weigh heavily in Congressional consideration of any future trade agreements

---

48 Steven Mufson, "Zoellick Wants Wealth Funds to Invest 1% in Africa," *Washington Post,* April 3, 2008.

49 From a global standpoint, successful completion of the World Trade Organization's Doha Round of trade negotiations, or a successor round, would probably provide more effective support for liberalization than any other trade agreement.

50 At the regional level, the U.S. Middle East Free Trade Area Initiative, started in 2003, seeks to establish a Middle East Free Trade Area (MEFTA) by 2013, see www.ustr.gov.

with Muslim countries, as long as those agreements include appropriate labor and environmental standards.

From a strategic standpoint, the U.S. should seek additional trade and investment agreements with countries and areas of critical importance to U.S. national security, where the needs for job creation are substantial and where there are reasonable prospects of success. These countries and areas include the Palestinian Territories, Lebanon, Egypt, and Pakistan. Iraq and Afghanistan are also high priorities for job creation, but their security environments and serious infrastructure problems require major governmental aid programs before public-private partnerships are likely to be effective.

Manage energy interdependence and diversify resources. Finally, the Leadership Group recognizes that many Americans want to reduce U.S. reliance on oil imports, including those from the Middle East. However, oil is a globally traded commodity. Acting alone, the U.S. has limited power to affect prices or suppliers. More fundamentally, our energy interdependence provides benefits as well as risks to the U.S. economy and to our national security.

The Leadership Group appreciates the numerous recommendations from experts and leaders during the past several years for the U.S. to more effectively manage energy interdependence by adopting a comprehensive national energy strategy.[51] Such a strategy should include, at a minimum: increasing and diversifying our energy resources, including oil, gas, renewables, and other alternatives, in the U.S. and abroad; embracing a greater commitment to energy efficiency; accelerating the development and adoption of new energy technologies; and reducing climate change risks from energy production and consumption.

As the U.S. seeks to diversify energy sources and suppliers, it is in our interest to work with oil-producing Muslim countries to help them develop a wider range of energy resources across a broader spectrum

---

51 See e.g. National Commission on Energy Policy, *Ending the Energy Stalemate: A Bipartisan Strategy to Meet America's Energy Challenges* (Washington, DC: National Commission on Energy Policy, 2004); Energy Security Leadership Council, *Recommendations to the Nation on Reducing U.S. Oil Dependence* (Washington, DC: Securing America's Future Energy, 2006).

of economic sectors. For example, Middle East oil producing countries may become major suppliers of solar power in the decades to come. Working together, we can make the transition to a more diverse and sustainable mix of energy resources, to our mutual benefit.

4   Improve mutual respect and understanding between Americans and Muslims around the world

- *Use public diplomacy to reinforce changes in policies and actions*

- *Dramatically expand cross-cultural education, people-to-people and interfaith exchange*

- *Promote greater depth and accuracy in news coverage and programming*

- *Invest in cultural diplomacy through arts and entertainment programs, to deepen mutual understanding and challenge stereotypes*

- *Involve the Muslim-American community as a bridge*

A chasm of misperception and misinformation divides Americans and Muslims around the world. This chasm could be bridged by a major expansion of efforts and resources devoted to improving mutual trust. There is a critical need for us to learn about our many common values, to overcome stereotypes and misperceptions, and to discuss areas of difference and disagreement with respect.

The Leadership Group recognizes that improving understanding alone will not transform relations; significant changes in policy direction and implementation by leaders in the U.S. and their counterparts in Muslim countries are necessary. Still, even if actions speak louder than words, they do not necessarily speak for themselves. Statements and symbolic actions by the President, the Secretary of State, and other senior Administration and Congressional leaders can have a significant and direct impact on the success of efforts to resolve conflict, improve governance, and promote economic development. More broadly, they can help to rebuild trust by clarifying the intent driving U.S. actions.

As with their actions, the statements of senior leaders will not be effective unless they are coordinated, amplified, and repeated by other officials, and diffused through nongovernmental and media channels. Given the perceptual and psychological barriers that have built up in many Muslim countries and communities during the last decade or more, promoting effective, two-way communication with key Muslim constituencies should be a major focus of U.S. public diplomacy and strategic communications.[52]

It is equally important to promote education, dialogue, and creative collaboration at the societal level, both as an end in itself and as a way to create more political opportunities for U.S. and Muslim leaders who want to improve relations. There are many promising initiatives on which to build, but their scale is still very small relative to the need. However, the U.S. government and the governments of Muslim majority countries need not only to increase funding, but also to change policies and regulations to make it far easier for Americans and Muslims in other countries to meet, talk, learn, and work together. Philanthropic, religious, and media organizations also need to make significant new investments to ensure that there is deep civic engagement to complement government-sponsored initiatives.

Use public diplomacy to reinforce changes in policies and actions. The incoming President and Secretary of State will have a critical window of opportunity to demonstrate a strong commitment to improving U.S.-Muslim relations, starting with the President's inaugural address

---

52 For an analysis of strategic communication challenges and many detailed institutional recommendations for the U.S. government and nongovernmental counterparts, see the January 2008 Report of the Defense Science Board Task Force on Strategic Communications (Washington, DC: Department of Defense, 2008).

and extending through the first several months of the Administration. The incoming Administration should use that window to take the following actions:

- Speak to the critical importance of improving relations with the global Muslim community in the inaugural address

- Immediately initiate high-level diplomacy for regional conflict resolution

- Convene a summit or high-level conference on job-creating economic development in the Middle East

- Affirm unambiguously the U.S. prohibition on all forms of torture

The President's inaugural address is closely watched around the world. It offers an ideal opportunity for stating clearly and forcefully the intention of the United States to improve its security, and its relations with Muslim countries and people around the world, by pursuing the four-pillar strategy outlined in this Report.

As discussed in Pillar 1, the President should elevate the use of diplomacy for conflict resolution by initiating a major and sustained diplomatic effort to resolve regional conflicts and promote security cooperation in the Middle East. In parallel, the President should convene a high-level forum to coordinate and accelerate economic reforms and investments across the Middle East. The President and other senior officials should seek high visibility for these initiatives, and communicate regularly about their progress, to demonstrate a significant change in course for the U.S. in the region.

It will be both symbolically and practically important to maintain high-level leadership, coordinate diplomatic and economic initiatives, and manage related efforts to improve governance and promote mutual respect and understanding (the need for high-level leadership and coordination is discussed in Section VI: Implementing the Strategy). Symbolically, governments and leaders around the world will be watching carefully to assess the extent to which the incoming Administration is committed to implementing a new policy framework.

Around the world, images and accounts of mistreatment of prisoners in Iraq, and at the Guantanamo Bay detention facility, have led many people to conclude that the U.S. has violated human rights and international norms in its counterinsurgency and counterterrorism operations. The current Administration has already indicated its desire to close the facility, and both Presidential candidates have committed to close it as well.[53] The June 2008 Supreme Court decision upholding the right of detainees to appeal their detention in Federal court has further eroded the rationale for such a facility. Assuming that the incoming Administration does act immediately to close the facility, the President should use the occasion to reaffirm the U.S. commitment not to use torture, and to abide by all of the its international commitments regarding the treatment of prisoners.

Beyond these immediate actions, the President, Administration, and Congressional leaders should seek, in all their public statements relating to Muslim countries and the global Muslim community, to be respectful of Islam as a religion, and to recognize the very strong complementarity of interests and values among the vast majority of Muslims around the world and Americans (including Muslim-Americans). The Administration should look for opportunities to participate in international discussions and initiatives to improve relations between Muslim and Western countries.

It is critically important not to provide additional ammunition to extremists by linking the term "Islam" or key tenets of the religion of Islam with the actions of extremist or terrorist groups. For example,

---

53 President Bush stated his desire to close the Guantanamo Bay detention facility in a Rose Garden press conference on June 14, 2006, transcript available at www.whitehouse.gov. Senator John McCain expressed his intention to close it in a CBS "60 Minutes" interview on April 8, 2007, transcript available at www.cbsnews.com. Senator Barack Obama called for its closure in an August 1, 2007 speech titled "The War We Need to Win," available at www.barackobama.com. Additionally, at a March 2008 meeting at the University of Georgia, five former Secretaries of State indicated that the detention facility should be closed, both because of its impact on the way the U.S. is seen around the world, and because it does not accord with U.S. values or laws. See Aaron Gould Sheinin, "Former Secretaries of State: Close Guantanamo," *Atlanta Journal-Constitution*, March 27, 2008.

the use of the term "jihadi" to describe extremists actually offers them a compliment in Islamic discourse, because jihad, in the sense of non-violent spiritual striving, is a sacred obligation of all Muslims. Terms like "Islamo-fascism" link the religion to a totalitarian political creed,

An Alliance of Civilizations to Build Bridges

Established at the United Nations in 2005 with the co-sponsorship of the Governments of Spain and Turkey, the Alliance of Civilizations (AoC) serves as a bridge builder, catalyst and facilitator to promote respect and understanding across cultures. It places a particular priority on relations between Western and predominantly Muslim populations, and works through the facilitation of political dialogue and the mobilization of cooperative projects in the fields of media, education, youth, and migration. At the First AoC Forum held in Madrid, Spain, in January 2008, several practical initiatives were launched, including Silatech and the AoC Media Fund. Silatech is a $100 million global youth employment initiative that is being piloted by corporate, governmental, nongovernmental, and multi-lateral agencies in six Arab countries and the AoC Media Fund. The AoC Media Fund has attracted an initial $10 million investment, and established partnerships with major Hollywood production, distribution, and talent agencies that seek to harness the power of mass media to address the urgent need of improving cross-cultural relations and understanding.

As of the writing of this Report, the AoC has gained the support of 89 UN member states, multilateral agencies, and international organizations that form the AoC "Group of Friends" at the UN. Among the group are many long-standing U.S. allies, including Australia, every member state of the EU, and predominantly Muslim countries in Africa, the Middle East, and Southeast Asia.

See the AoC Web site at www.unaoc.org, the Silatech Web site at www.silatech.com, and the AoC Media Fund Web site at www.aocmediafund.org.

an implication that the vast majority of Muslims around the world find grossly untrue and offensive.

Instead, U.S. leaders should seek both to acknowledge and respect the religious tenets of Islam and the dignity of Muslims around the world, while condemning extremist violence as an affront to human rights that has no legitimacy among the vast majority of Muslims.

Beyond government leaders' statements and symbolic actions, there is an immense need and opportunity for improvements in U.S. citizens' understanding of and respect for Islam and Muslim cultures, and conversely in Muslim citizens understanding of and respect for American values and institutions. The Leadership Group calls for a dramatic expansion in societal respect and understanding through scaling up and deepening of mutual education, dialogue, exchange, and media coverage.

Dramatically expand cross-cultural education. Education can occur in schools and universities through a range of relevant courses, and through public-education events, faith communities, cultural events, and the media. Topics for education and dialogue could range from the common roots and values of Judaism, Christianity, and Islam, to the political history of the Muslim world and the lively, parallel debates in the U.S. and many Muslim countries on the appropriate role of religion in politics.

The U.S. government, together with educational, philanthropic, and business organizations, should substantially expand present commitments to academic and professional education on Muslim history, religion, and culture, and on issues in U.S.-Muslim relations. Excellent curricula and resources for teaching already exist.[54] The Federal government could provide incentives for teacher training, to encourage teachers to integrate this information into social studies, world history, U.S. history, current events, and comparative politics courses.

---

54 For example, the World Affairs Council Global Classroom program has developed "Beyond Islam: Understanding the Muslim World," which includes curriculum units, teacher training, and a youth summit. The curriculum materials are available for download at www.world-affairs. org.

American Mountain Climber Brings Education and Opportunity to Remote Areas

In 1993, Greg Mortenson wandered alone into a remote Pakistani village after a failed mountaineering attempt. His stay endeared him to the people of that region and he left inspired to improve their children's access to education. With assistance from Swiss Dr. Jean Hoerni in 1996, Mortenson founded the Central Asia Institute (CAI). Since that time, the CAI has established 64 schools in Pakistan and Afghanistan that have enrolled more than 25,000 students, a high percentage of them girls. The organization's direct focus on improving literacy and education in the most inaccessible regions has been widely acclaimed as a successful model of development and peacemaking. For example, Massachusetts Congressman John Tierney commented, "Let us fight terrorism with textbooks and blackboards now, rather than with more bullets and bombs later."

For more information, see the CAI Web site at www.ikat.org. Mortenson's own story can be read in the best-selling memoir, Three Cups of Tea (New York: Viking Press, 2006).

At the university and post-graduate levels, the Federal government has already expanded funding for Arabic language study and regional studies focused on the Middle East, South and Southeast Asia. However, both government and nongovernmental leaders need to provide more substantial incentives for teaching and learning Arabic, Farsi, Urdu, Turkish, and Bahasa Indonesia, and for undergraduate and postgraduate study of Muslim national and regional cultures, histories, and politics.

Overall, the U.S. needs an education program comparable in scale to the post-Sputnik U.S. commitment to math and science education. The National Defense Education Act of 1958 committed the equivalent (in today's dollars) of more than $7 billion to meet the challenge posed by Soviet space research. The current challenge calls for an equivalent commitment to education on Islam and Muslims, sustained over a decade or more, focusing on teacher training and curriculum in middle and high schools, and colleges.

It is equally important for the U.S. to expand its commitment to fund basic education (literacy and numeracy) in Muslim countries, and to support teaching and learning about other cultures as part of the curriculum. The U.S. should not impose its view of what should be taught about other cultures in Muslim countries' schools. Nonetheless, the U.S. should use dialogue and advocacy to promote balanced presentation of historical, political, and cultural issues, and to put an end to teaching that advocates violence. When advocating educational reforms, the U.S. government and nongovernmental agencies should seek to the fullest extent possible to work through multilateral organizations and/or with government partners who share their views on core educational principles.

Expand international exchanges to build respect and understanding.
There is clear social-science evidence that well-structured contact and dialogue between members of conflicting groups can reduce prejudice and increase mutual respect and understanding.[55] There are also strategic, cultural, and economic gains for the U.S. when bright young Muslims, who will some day be leaders in their own countries, come to the U.S. for their education.

Organizations involved in cross-cultural student, cultural, professional, or community exchanges, and U.S. businesses with operations in Muslim countries, should substantially scale up their efforts to promote direct contact among citizens and leaders from the U.S. and Muslim countries. For example, the Brookings Institution has proposed a $50 million fund to support 10,000 Global Service Fellowships per year.[56]

---

55 Thomas F. Pettigrew, University of California, Santa Cruz, and Linda R. Tropp, Boston College, "Summary of *A Meta-Analytic Test and Reformulation of Intergroup Contact Theory*," n.d., available at www.bc.edu.

56 See David L. Caprara, John Bridgeland and Harris Wofford, "Global Service Fellowships: Building Bridges through American Volunteers," The Brookings Institution Policy Brief #160, March

Exchanges should target education, media, labor, military, religious, and community leaders, because of their potential impact as opinion makers. Exchanges should also include musicians, artists, and others who can have a major effect on public perceptions and opinions.

To ensure that these exchanges are fully reciprocal, the U.S. Department of Homeland Security should reexamine visa-granting procedures for applicants from Muslim countries who are participating in reputable programs, to see if application time, cost, and rejection rates can be brought down without compromising security. As an alternative to face-to-face contact, Internet-based videoconferencing can provide a lower-cost means of communication with potentially far-reaching impacts. Educational, professional, and cultural organizations should expand the use of videoconferencing for learning and dialogue.[57]

Use interfaith dialogue and action to promote mutual respect among the Abrahamic faiths. Since 9/11, there have been a number of efforts by leaders of the Abrahamic faiths (Judaism, Christianity, and Islam) to demonstrate their mutual respect, solidarity, and commitment to nonviolence.[58] The Leadership Group strongly endorses these efforts, and recommends that denominational leaders of all faiths—and in particular, the three monotheistic faiths—continue and expand their efforts. One goal should be to increase the visibility of respectful interfaith discussion by holding well-publicized dialogues with mainstream media coverage in the U.S., the Middle East, and Asia.

Interfaith discussions of committed partners at the leadership level

---

2007 (Washington, DC: Brookings Institution, 2007).

57 The value of videoconferencing to build bridges has been demonstrated by the U.S.-Iran Working Group on Health Science Cooperation, which has orchestrated a series of successful video-conferences linking medical professionals in the U.S. and Iran.

58 For example, the National Interreligious Leadership Initiative for Peace in the Middle East unites the voices of prominent religious leaders of more than 25 Jewish, Christian, and Muslim national organizations in a collaborative effort to "mobilize broad support for active, fair, and firm U.S. leadership in pursuit of Arab-Israeli-Palestinian peace," see www.nili-mideastpeace. org. For more information on interfaith initiatives, groups, events, and trends in the U.S. and internationally, see the database at the Interfaith Initiative of the Pluralism Project at Harvard University at www.pluralism.org.

Building Bridges Through Web-Based Video Dialogue

The Soliya Connect Program exemplifies how students from the Middle East, North Africa, the United States, and Europe can successfully bridge the cultural divide. For one semester, multinational groups meet weekly via an Internet-based videoconferencing system to jointly explore their different communities and the broader relationship between the West and the Arab/Muslim world. With help from skilled cross-cultural facilitators, the students exchange views on such diverse issues as the role of religion in public life, the status of women in their societies, and the conflict in the Middle East. They write joint op-eds and create joint news videos to receive course credit. Upon program completion, virtually all participants express greater knowledge, a more nuanced understanding, and a better appreciation of commonalities with their counterparts. To date, the program has brought together more than 1,000 students at a relatively low cost, with gains in knowledge, understanding, and lasting friendships.

See the Soliya Web site at www.soliya.net.

will not, however, be sufficient to change the views of millions of lay believers. Expanded efforts to connect lay believers through Web-based as well as face-to-face dialogue, and through action projects, will be critical for promoting broad-based and sustained respect and understanding.

International cooperation should not be limited to explicitly interfaith efforts. Organizations focused on youth actions, social service projects, and/or volunteerism, also have an important role to play in building interfaith respect and understanding. International volunteer service that leads to greater interfaith understanding can empower U.S. volunteers while building global peace and stability. Social service projects—with Jews, Christians, and Muslims working side-by-side

Walking the Abraham Path

The Abraham Path is a route of cultural tourism that retraces the journey made by Abraham through the heart of the Middle East some 4,000 years ago. The Abraham Path Initiative honors the shared cultural heritage of Muslim, Jewish, and Christian communities by linking a single itinerary of ancient sites associated with Abraham and his family. To be launched in 2008, the initiative seeks to serve as an intercultural meeting place inspiring respect and understanding among people around the world. It aims to be an economic catalyst creating sustainable development through responsible tourism, and to promote positive media focus by highlighting the unique heritage and hospitality of the region.

See the Abraham Path Initiative Web site at www.abrahampath.org.

to serve those in need—are a powerful way to break down barriers between the communities. Initiatives such as the Interfaith Youth Core have demonstrated the sustainable benefits of empowering youth across cultures and religions to work together to serve others, to the betterment of their respective and shared communities.[59] Cooperative action can also occur around faith-based tourism or a shared appreciation of history.

Promote greater depth and accuracy in news coverage and programming. Though there is a great deal of media coverage on tensions in U.S.-Muslim relations, the primary coverage is breaking news about violent conflicts in the Middle East.[60] The Leadership Group recognizes

---

59 See the Interfaith Youth Core Web site at www.ifyc.org.

60 An analysis of U.S. TV news between January 2007 and March 2008 found that Islam was the most reported-on religion, and that the majority of statements about Islam were negative. The same analysis found that 58 percent of protagonists associated with Islam were militants, while the majority of protagonists associated with Christianity were religious leaders. See Media Tenor, "Cycle of Violence Drives Coverage of Islam," Report prepared for the Western-Islamic World

Muslim Religious Leaders Seek Common Ground with Christians

In September 2007, under the patronage of King Abdullah II of Jordan and The Royal Aal al-Bayt Institute for Islamic Thought, a group of 138 Muslim scholars and clerics of all sects and denominations signed an open letter titled "A Common Word between Us and You." The letter, addressed to Christians in general and leaders of the world's churches in particular, points out the critical need for peace between Muslims and Christians. It recognizes that there is fundamental common ground between Muslim and Christian beliefs: in the unity of God, the love of God, and the love of the neighbor. It calls for building future interfaith dialogue and understanding on the basis of these shared beliefs. The spirit of the letter was widely welcomed by the Christian faith community, though some questioned whether Muslims and Christians have the same theological beliefs about the unity of God. The letter and the response have sparked ongoing dialogue within and across the two communities.

See the "A Common Word" Web site a www.acommonword.com.

that the news business is a competitive enterprise, and that there are trade-offs between providing in-depth coverage and maintaining ratings. Without adding substantially to the cost of coverage, news media could provide more diverse perspectives on breaking news and ongoing stories.

In particular, U.S. news Web sites could provide more extensive links to commentators based in Muslim countries, and Muslim media Web sites could provide more links to commentators based in the U.S. Discussion between the production and editorial staffs of major U.S. news media and counterparts in Muslim national and regional markets

Dialogue of the World Economic Forum, April 2008, available at www.mediachannel.org.

about diversity and depth of coverage could also be productive. In the U.S., news media could expand their coverage of Muslims in non-conflictual contexts, including charitable and civic organizations, fundraising events and cultural activities, while simultaneously giving more publicity to Muslim condemnations of terrorism and extremism.[61]

Whatever initiatives are taken by news media to provide more innovative coverage, it is important that they be voluntary and clearly separate from governmental public diplomacy, and from soft or hard censorship. For example, leading U.S. and international associations of journalists and schools of journalism could expand their efforts to convene dialogues on both sensitive issues and the coverage of those issues in the U.S. and in Muslim media markets.

Invest in cultural diplomacy through arts and entertainment programs, to deepen mutual understanding and challenge stereotypes. Entertainment media can make important contributions to popular perceptions of conflict and the potential for respectful coexistence.[62] Entertainment programming aimed at building respect and understanding does not have to be overt to be effective. In the U.S., TV series could move beyond high-conflict terrorism dramas to portray other issues in U.S.-Muslim relations, or simply to incorporate more Muslim characters into regular programming.[63]

The arts can play a critical role in increasing respect and understanding between people in the U.S. and the global Muslim community. The performing and visual arts have a unique capacity to educate and

---

61 As recommended by The Chicago Council on Global Affairs, Task Force on Muslim American Civic and Political Engagement, in its 2007 report "Strengthening America: The Civic and Political Integration of Muslim Americans."

62 Search for Common Ground, a Washington- and Brussels-based conflict resolution organization, uses the tools of popular culture to communicate messages of tolerance and reconciliation in divided societies. It produces innovative TV, radio, and musical and Internet programming to promote changes in attitudes and behaviors.

63 The Brookings Project on U.S. Relations with the Islamic World, in partnership with Unity Productions Foundation and One Nation Media Initiative, is developing a new "Hollywood Engagement Initiative" in order to provide valuable resources and accurate information on Islam and Muslims for the U.S. entertainment community. Leadership Group member Dalia Mogahed, personal communication, May 2008.

Mainstream TV Shows Challenge Stereotypes

Canadian Broadcasting Corporation's TV show *Little Mosque on the Prairie* attracted 2.1 million viewers on its series premiere in January 2007. The series explores the humorous side of being a Muslim in post-9/11 North America, while breaking through stereotypes about Muslims as extremists. While extremists seek to convince other Muslims that the West disrespects their community and values, this show portrays Muslim life in Canada as something worthy of respect and appreciation.

In the same month, the Middle East Broadcasting Centre (MBC) network aired the first segment of Layalina Productions' *On the Road in America*, a reality travelogue tracing the journey of three Arab students across the United States. The 12-part series, which garnered 4.5 million viewers per episode across the Arab world, aims to help overcome mutual stereotypes between Arabs and Americans by showing the students interacting with the communities they visit.

See the Little Mosque on the Prairie *Web site at www.cbc.ca and learn more about* On the Road in America *at www.layalina.tv.*

humanize people through their emotional impact. For example, the Pakistani rock band Junoon has had a major impact on both intercultural and international relations between India and Pakistan.[64] As reported by the Arts and Culture Task Force of the Brookings Institution, Muslim and American artists want closer connections with their counterparts, to build cross-cultural understanding through artistic endeavors. There is a range of opportunities for supporting artistic cooperation and interchange through new public-private, cross-cultural partnerships.[65]

---

64 See e.g. "Pakistan's Political Pop Stars," *BBC News Online,* July 12, 2003.

65 Cynthia P. Schneider, Kristina Nelson, Mohammed Youssry, "Mightier than the Sword: Arts and Culture in the U.S.-Islamic World Relationship," Brooking Institution, Arts and Culture Task Force,

Illuminating Islam Through the Arts

New York University Center for Dialogues: Islamic World-U.S.-The West, Asia Society, and the Brooklyn Academy of Music are organizing, under the title *Illuminating Islam,* a multidisciplinary arts festival and themed conference on a scale that is unprecedented in the United States. It will be held in New York from June 5 through 14, 2009. *Illuminating Islam* will gather artists, writers, poets, scholars, religious leaders, and policy makers from the U.S. and around the world for a range of programs designed to attract wide-scale popular attention. Mainstream American and Muslim communities will be drawn together to experience the richness and diversity of the Islamic world. The conference will explore new avenues for engagement between the Western and Islamic worlds using culture as a lens. A comprehensive media strategy will ensure broad dissemination of the festival and conference.

Learn more about Illuminating Islam *at www.centerfordialogues.org.*

Involve the Muslim-American community as a bridge. The Muslim-American community can act as a unique bridge between the U.S. and Muslim countries and people in all the areas described earlier—education, exchange, dialogue, cooperative action, and media. There are prominent Muslim-Americans in many professions, in the arts and culture, and in faith and public interest organizations. Many are concerned both about their fellow Americans' misperceptions of Islam and the global Muslim community, and about widespread misunderstandings of American culture and politics among Muslims overseas.[66]

Several ongoing efforts and groups profiled earlier seek to support Muslim-American leaders as emissaries and bridge figures within the U.S. and in Muslim countries. The Muslim-American community

---

paper prepared for presentation at the U.S.-Islamic World Forum, Doha, February 16-18, 2008.

66 See e.g. Lisa Miller, "American Dreamers," *Newsweek,* July 30, 2007.

Sports Diplomacy Shrinks the Cross-Cultural Divide

Sports has long been recognized as a powerful medium for building trust between nations. The United Nations Inter-Agency Task Force on Sport for Development and Peace has also strongly endorsed its importance as a diplomatic tool. One example is Search for Common Ground's (SFCG's) 1998 "Wrestling Diplomacy" initiative. SFCG assisted the American wrestling team to compete in the international Takhti Cup tournament in Iran. The team was the first U.S. delegation to visit Iran since the Iranian Revolution. Using the popularity of wrestling in Iran, the exchange became a major accomplishment in creating an atmosphere of shared respect. Praised by both governments, the initiative has served as a model for other sports exchanges between the two countries, including a return trip to Iran and the winning of the Takhti Cup by the American wrestling team in January 2007.

See the SFCG Web site at www.sfcg.org, the Web site of the U.S. Department of State at exchanges.state.gov, and the Web site of the United Nations Inter-Agency Task Force on Sport for Development and Peace at www.un.org.

could make an even more significant contribution, but needs greater recognition and integration into governmental and philanthropic initiatives. Regular meetings on Muslim countries' relations with Administration foreign policy officials, and with members of Congress, could help to communicate their insights and make them even more effective as bridge builders.

VI.

Implementing the Strategy

IMPLEMENTING THE STRATEGY proposed in this Report will require a sustained and coordinated effort across a wide range of public and private institutions. There are already successes to point to in each area, but the nation has not yet formed an overarching vision for improving U.S.-Muslim relations, clarified the key elements of the strategy and their interdependence, or made political, financial, or human resource commitments equal to the challenge.

Leadership from the highest levels of government is of paramount importance to ensure a highly visible launch, sustained momentum, and buy-in and support across government agencies. The strategy requires strong leadership to closely coordinate diplomatic, political, and economic initiatives involving many agencies over a period of years.

A long-term strategy for improving relations with the global Muslim community poses serious challenges for the U.S. government. Traditionally, political leaders find it difficult, except in the most dramatic crises, to commit resources and maintain attention over a time span and at a scale equal to the need. For a multifaceted strategy like the one we recommend, there are additional institutional challenges because of the need to coordinate and ensure accountability across U.S. foreign policy, security, economic, intelligence, and military institutions, and across multiple regions.

As one tool for coordination, it may be useful to prioritize key Muslim countries and governments for cross-cutting integration of diplomatic, political, and economic engagement. Our short list of such countries and governments would include Iraq, Iran, Afghanistan, Pakistan, Egypt, the Palestinian Authority, Turkey, and Indonesia.

It may also be useful to create high-level positions in the National Security Council, the State Department, and USAID to coordinate and drive the strategy. Britain, the Netherlands, and Switzerland have senior foreign policy officials tasked to look to the broader relationship between each of their countries and Muslim communities globally. They play an invaluable role in advising more narrowly focused policy making bodies.[1]

To coordinate the activities of a wide range of private actors while maintaining their separation from the government, we recommend that leading business, educational, cultural, media, philanthropic, and faith organizations expand existing forums for discussion of U.S.-Muslim relations, and create new ones, with outreach to counterparts in Muslim countries.

Managing the Risks of Terrorism and Counterterrorism

During the next several years, this strategy has the potential to shrink the base of public and leadership support for Muslim extremist groups. If so, it will reduce—though not eliminate—the need for U.S. counterterrorism and counterinsurgency operations. People around the world are acutely sensitive to civilian casualties and human rights abuses caused by U.S. military and counterterrorism operations. The American public seeks to restore the moral standing of the U.S. in the world at large. For these and other reasons, it is essential that U.S. operations

---

1   Leadership Group member Shamil Idriss, personal communication, June 2008.

minimize risks to civilians, respect the rights of suspects and prisoners, and not condone or ignore abuses by the security services of cooperating governments. Current U.S. counterinsurgency thinking strongly supports this approach.[2]

The need for tightly targeted use of force will be most acute if there is another major attack on the U.S., causing hundreds or thousands of casualties. The public and political pressure to retaliate immediately on likely perpetrators and their supporters will be intense. It will be critical for the U.S. government and leaders in both political parties to respond firmly and proportionately based on the hardest possible evidence.

To strengthen the legitimacy and the ultimate effectiveness of the response, it will also be critical for the U.S. to work visibly and collaboratively with government, religious, and civic leaders across the Muslim world and beyond, most of whom will condemn any such attack. It will be in our interest and theirs to work jointly in gathering, reviewing, and validating the evidence. It will also be in our joint interest to consult them on the response, without compromising the speed and secrecy necessary for success. Together, we can demonstrate that the threat and the response are not only American but truly global concerns.

---

2   See esp. Gompert, Gordon et al., *War by Other Means,* op. cit., pp. 62-77.

VII.

Recommendations for Leaders and Citizens

THE LEADERSHIP GROUP strongly urges our nation's political, defense and military, business, philanthropic, faith, news media, and educational leaders to begin implementing the strategy presented in this Report by taking the following actions.

Presidential Candidates

While acknowledging the need for counterterrorism operations, candidates should speak to the importance of a comprehensive strategy for improving U.S. relations with Muslim countries and communities, and use the four-pillar approach proposed here as a basis for policy on U.S.-Muslim relations.

Candidates should pledge to revamp our approach to U.S.-Muslim relations immediately upon taking office, to set a new tone in relations with Muslim countries and peoples, and to shift U.S. public perceptions of the challenges and opportunities that stand before us.

The Next U.S. President

The next U.S. President and Administration must provide immediate and sustained leadership on improving U.S.-Muslim relations. We recommend that the next President take these steps:

- Speak to the critical importance of improving relations with the global Muslim community in his 2009 inaugural address

- Take key actions immediately to demonstrate a commitment to improving relations, including:

  - Immediately organizing a whole-of-government effort, with Presidential leadership, to define and implement a strategy for improving relations with key Muslim countries and communities

  - Immediately re-affirming the U.S. commitment to prohibit all forms of torture

- Within the first three months of the Administration, initiate a major and sustained diplomatic effort to resolve regional conflicts and promote security cooperation in the Middle East, giving top priority to engagement with Iran and permanent resolution of the Israeli-Palestinian conflict

- Within the first six months of the Administration, co-convene a business-government summit on economic reform, growth, and job creation in the Middle East to accelerate current reform and investment initiatives

- Work with leaders in Congress, educational, cultural and philanthropic institutions in the U.S., and counterparts in Muslim countries, to create and fund a global initiative for teaching, learning, and exchange among citizens in the U.S. and Muslim countries

- Co-convene forums on U.S.-Muslim relations with business, faith, philanthropic, and media leaders from the U.S. and other countries, and create new platforms for action, making special efforts to involve Muslim-American leaders

Members of Congress

Members of Congress should support and allocate resources to each of the four pillars in the following ways:

- Support sustained U.S. diplomatic efforts on the major Middle East conflicts along the lines outlined in this Report

- Make progress on political and economic reform a key criterion for allocating military and economic assistance, and for supporting trade and investment in Muslim countries[1]

- Make it easier for quasi- and nongovernmental organizations in the U.S. to work with a wider range of political and social movements in Muslim countries, including nonviolent Islamist movements

- Provide incentives for economic reform, and for U.S. and multilateral investment in job creation in Muslim countries, through enterprise funds, export promotion, and trade agreements

- Support the establishment of Economic Support Funds in key areas of conflict, such as Iraq and Pakistan

- Dramatically expand funds for U.S. secondary and university education on the Muslim world, and for programs to educate students across the Muslim world about the U.S.; a commitment of several billion dollars within the U.S., and an equivalent amount for Muslim countries,

---

1   See for example the legislation introduced by Senators Biden and Lugar in July 2008, Enhanced Partnership with Pakistan Act of 2008, op. cit.

over a five–year period, could have a very significant impact

- Fund a substantial expansion of student, professional and cultural exchange programs, with smarter targeting of visa restrictions to enable Muslims who pose low security risk, especially journalists, business people, and religious leaders, to enter the U.S. more easily

- Support enhanced consular representation in Muslim countries, and consider a re-balancing of security interests and interests in exchange when reviewing visa policy

- Increase Congressional understanding of the ways in which the choice of words to describe issues in U.S.-Muslim relations can be inflammatory and detrimental to the goal of improving relations

Defense and Military Leaders

Defense and military leaders should:

- Broaden foreign student participation from Muslim countries at U.S. military service academies, and at U.S. officer and noncommissioned officer (NCO) training centers

- Deepen military exercise, training, and exchange programs, consistent with U.S. national security priorities, with Muslim countries where better coordination and execution of civil-military counterinsurgency and counterterrorism efforts is a U.S. priority

- Update appropriate doctrinal manuals (for example, the U.S. Army Counterinsurgency Field Manual, FM 3-24) that relate to stability operations in the developing world, to ensure consideration of the full range of "non-kinetic" (that is, nonmilitary) elements of power, including the private sector; and ensure that non-kinetic elements are a central part of combatant commanders' regional planning and exercise schedules

- Ensure consistent and universal understanding throughout the uniform services of the proper treatment of prisoners and enemy combatants; all service members must understand the importance of adhering to international norms in this vital area affecting global perceptions

Business and Investment Leaders

Business and investment leaders should:

- Communicate to U.S. political leaders that improving U.S.-Muslim relations is critical to the long-term health and stability of the U.S. and global economies

- In Muslim countries with current business operations and/or new opportunities for investment, work through business associations to seek improvements in the business climate (for example, transparency, rule of law, and regulation), and design operations to maximize local employment, skill-building, and enterprise growth throughout the value chain

Philanthropic Institutions and Development Agencies

Philanthropic institutions and development agencies should increase support for:

- Muslim-led organizations (based in the U.S. and abroad) that promote political and economic reform in Muslim countries

- Job training and employment programs targeting youth in Muslim countries

- Teaching and learning about Muslim history, culture, and current events in U.S. and Muslim country schools and universities

- Student, cultural, professional, and interfaith dialogues and exchanges between the U.S. and Muslim countries

- Journalism and media productions aimed at providing balanced, in-depth coverage of controversial issues in U.S.-Muslim relations

Educators

Educators should:

- Significantly expand the time devoted to teaching and learning about Muslim history, culture, and current events in middle and secondary schools and universities

- Support professional development for teaching about the Muslim world

- Use the Internet to create structured dialogue between students in the U.S. and Muslim countries

- Promote student and teacher exchanges with counterparts in Muslim countries

Christian, Muslim, Jewish, and other Faith Leaders

Christian, Muslim, Jewish, and other faith leaders should:

- Actively and visibly promote interfaith dialogue, respect, and understanding through public statements, religious education, interfaith convocations, and celebrations

- Make clear, public statements condemning acts of violence by those claiming religious justification

- Help build public support for constructive engagement among Muslims, Christians, and Jews based upon shared religious values; religious leaders can use their influence to inspire those in their traditions to act consistently with the values of tolerance and inclusion common to the Abrahamic faiths

- Provide guidance and mentorship specifically for youth, and integrate them in interfaith efforts so that they develop tolerance and respect for other faith traditions

News and Entertainment Media Owners

News and entertainment media owners should:

- Provide funding, professional development opportunities, and career incentives for in-depth reporting on U.S.-Muslim relations

- Institutionalize contact and dialogue with counterparts in the Muslim world (especially those involved in satellite broadcasting and major newspapers), to encourage higher quality coverage of controversial issues, culture, and society

- Expand coverage on everyday activities of Muslims, especially in the context of charitable and civic organizations, fundraising events, or cultural activities

- Give more publicity to Muslim condemnations of extremism and terrorism, and enrich coverage on Muslim issues by citing credible Muslim leaders and constituents

- Explore, research, and create nuanced and accurate film and television portrayals of Muslim characters, reflecting the diversity and complexity of this faith community

All Americans

American citizens should:

- Contact their elected representatives and ask whether they have seen this Report, and how they are acting to address the issues raised in the Report

- Contact their local media and seek accurate and unbiased coverage of U.S.-Muslim issues in order to promote a well-informed democracy

- Participate in interfaith dialogues in their churches, synagogues, mosques or other faith communities

- Ask their school districts what educators are doing to invest in students' global education, especially education on Muslim majority countries where the U.S. is heavily engaged

- Actively support educational exchange programs in their communities that involve Muslim students from overseas

VIII.

Conclusion

THE LEADERSHIP GROUP believes that now is the time for a national discussion on relations with the global Muslim community, and for action to implement a new strategy for U.S.-Muslim engagement. Violent extremism in the name of Islam poses a serious security threat not only to the U.S. but also (indeed, primarily) to Muslim populations and countries themselves. The much-publicized divide between the U.S. and the larger Muslim world may be deep, but it is not irreconcilable. There is a convergence of values and interests among the vast majority of Muslims and Americans that provides a starting point for relationships based on mutual confidence and respect.

Implementing these recommendations will not eliminate the risk of terrorist attacks on the U.S. Nonetheless, if our commitment is broad, deep, and sustained, the new strategy will reshape U.S.-Muslim relations in ways that lead to much greater mutual respect and understanding; improve the lives of many millions of Muslims around the world; and make the U.S. and the world safer.

Annex: Causes of Tension in U.S.-Muslim Relations

THERE IS A WIDE RANGE of views among Americans and across the Muslim world about why and how relations have deteriorated. What follows is an attempt to present key events and trends on which there is relatively broad agreement, while acknowledging important differences in perspective on key issues.

The conflict with Muslim extremists, and widespread Muslim frustration with the U.S., did not begin on September 11, 2001. Since the end of World War II, the U.S. has played an increasingly important and sometimes controversial role in Muslim countries across North Africa, the Middle East and Asia. Though the U.S. did not have a single policy or strategy for relations with Muslim countries, three concerns were significant in shaping relations:

- Creating and maintaining alliances with Muslim countries' governments to contain Soviet influence

- Maintaining the stability and security of Middle East oil production and supply

- Supporting the state of Israel while seeking to resolve the Arab-Israeli conflict

Given U.S. concerns, the Middle East has been a primary focus of U.S. policy and strategy through most of the postwar period. Other predominantly Muslim regions and countries gained attention when they became flashpoints in the Cold War conflict (for example, Afghanistan and Pakistan after the 1979 Soviet invasion of Afghanistan).

Starting in the late 1940s, Muslim countries gained independence from colonial control. Most of the new rulers were secular and nationalist in their ideologies, and they tightly controlled politics and economic activity.

The U.S. made three decisions during the 1940s and 1950s that had long-term impact on Muslim perceptions and interests. First, in 1948, in the face of widespread opposition from Arab states and Muslim publics, the U.S. recognized the new state of Israel as a homeland for the Jewish people and a potential democratic ally in the Middle East. Second, in the early 1950s, the U.S. became directly involved in toppling the democratically elected, left-leaning prime minister of Iran, and installing a new Shah (king) allied to and dependent on the U.S. Both decisions sparked widespread anger in Muslim countries and communities. Third, in 1956, the Eisenhower administration's intervention to end the Suez crisis made the U.S. the dominant Western power in the Middle East, replacing Britain and France. Eisenhower declared that the U.S. would use its military and economic influence in the region to fight Communism. Many Muslims welcomed the U.S. intervention against the former colonial powers, but were wary of the growing U.S. presence.

Over the next 30 years, in Muslim countries from Morocco to Indonesia, the U.S. was to become increasingly influential and controversial as a provider of military and economic aid, as a source of political and diplomatic support for allied governments, and as an obstacle to political movements that challenged those governments.

In the 1960s, secular, nationalist governments in the Middle East and elsewhere in the Muslim world began to lose legitimacy. Many citizens saw them as military and diplomatic failures (particularly following Israel's traumatic defeat of Arab armies in the Six-Day War of 1967); many citizens also became intensely frustrated with the lack of economic or political opportunity.

During the 1970s, "political Islam," based on the idea that governments should rule according to Islamic principles (*Sharia*), became increasingly popular in the Middle East, South and Southeast Asia as a way to express opposition to authoritarian governments. Saudi Arabia became a leader in supporting and exporting a radical interpretation of *Sharia*, while remaining a close U.S. ally. In 1979, Iran's revolution overthrew the Shah, and offered a new model of political Islam based on direct rule by the clergy and hostile to what its leaders perceived as U.S. domination in the Middle East. The hostage crisis and the rise to power of Ayatollah Khomeini saw the end of U.S. diplomatic relations with Iran, and the beginning of a thirty-year period of heightened tensions.

During the 1980s, Muslim groups attacked the U.S. in several places, though most of the groups opposing the U.S. in this period were motivated by nationalist or pan-Arabist rather than Islamist ideology. In the same period, the U.S. (working closely with Pakistan and Saudi Arabia) supported the Afghan *mujahideen* in their struggle against Soviet occupation. The U.S. also supported Saddam Hussein's secular regime in its war with Iran, primarily to contain the spread of what the U.S. perceived as Iran's dangerous ideology and influence in the Middle East.

In the 1990s, several factors strained U.S. relations with Muslim countries and peoples. One was the Gulf War with Saddam Hussein. Most Americans saw the war as a legitimate and limited military effort to expel Saddam Hussein's forces from Kuwait and destroy his capacity to threaten his neighbors. The governments of many Muslim countries joined or supported the international coalition formed to oust Iraq's forces from Kuwait. Some Muslims, however, believed the U.S. had deliberately created a situation that justified an attack on Iraq as an excuse for dramatically increasing the U.S. military presence in the region. They were angered by their own governments' support for action against Iraq.

After the Gulf War, the U.S. expanded its military bases in Saudi Arabia, the country with the holiest sites in Islam. The bases became a focus of resentment among some Saudis and more widely among politically activist Muslims. So did international sanctions against Iraq, which many Muslims saw as hurting only civilians. As the Oslo peace process between Israel and the Palestinians broke down in the late 1990s, hostility to Israel and the U.S. intensified across the Middle East.

In the unsettled post-Cold War period, there was a strong wave of political opposition to authoritarian governments in the Middle East and in Central Asian countries and regions. Locally-based, sometimes loosely connected Islamist movements opposed the governments of Algeria, Egypt, Tajikistan, Uzbekistan, and Russian-controlled Chechnya. In some cases opposition was political and peaceful, and in other cases it was violent.

Muslim extremist movements were not successful in toppling any of these governments during the 1990s. As a result, some began to shift their strategy toward attacking the U.S. and other Western nations. Al-Qaeda affiliates were involved in attacks on the World Trade Center in 1993, U.S. embassies in East Africa in 1998, and the U.S.S. *Cole* in 2000. Their core justification for attacking the U.S. was to free the Muslim world—particularly the Arab lands that house Islam's sacred sites—from what they saw as Western domination. Pushing the West out of Muslim lands was to be the first step toward overthrowing the governments they saw as illegitimate, and establishing "true" Islamic states.

When the Taliban came to power in Afghanistan in the mid-1990s, Afghanistan became the primary training base for al-Qaeda and allied groups. Al-Qaeda's top leaders established ties with Muslim extremist groups in Egypt, Saudi Arabia, Pakistan, Indonesia, Malaysia, the Philippines, and Western Europe. The U.S. sought to disrupt al-Qaeda, but was not successful in preventing the 9/11 attacks.[1]

In retrospect, there were many, complex tensions in U.S.-Muslim relations before 9/11. Out of these tensions grew an increasingly sophisticated and dangerous network of Muslim extremist groups hostile to the U.S. American responses to Muslim extremists before 9/11 had mixed effects on their ability to organize and operate, and on public opinion about the U.S. in the Muslim world. A number of economic and political trends after the end of the Cold War—particularly the widespread sense that the Muslim world was falling further behind in a globalizing world—contributed to anti-U.S. sentiment.[2]

In the past seven years, tensions have increased dramatically as the cycle of attack, response, and mistrust has intensified. Today, the U.S. has no easy way to determine its best course of action. Nonetheless, it seems clear that the U.S. needs to develop a more comprehensive strategy to improve relations with Muslim countries and communities, while simultaneously seeking to reduce the risk of attacks in the U.S. and in other countries.

---

1   *The 9/11 Commission Report: Final Report of the National Commission on Terrorist Attacks Upon the United States* (New York: W.W. Norton, 2004) reviews and assesses these efforts in great detail.

2   See for example Wright, *The Looming Tower,* op. cit.

Acknowledgments

FIRST AND FOREMOST, we recognize the Leadership Group on U.S.-Muslim Engagement, whose members have generously donated time and knowledge over the past two years, providing in-depth interviews, attending multi-day meetings, reviewing drafts of the Report, making themselves available for multiple consultations, and helping with outreach to a wide range of constituencies.

Within the Leadership Group itself, several members have made extraordinary contributions. Stephen Heintz, President of the Rockefeller Brothers Fund, has been a guiding light, providing counsel and encouragement. Rockefeller Brothers Fund also hosted the initial meeting of the Leadership Group at its Pocantico Conference Center and has provided initial and oing financial support.

Special thanks are due Paul Brest, President of the William and Flora Hewlett Foundation, for supporting our work with generous financial assistance and guidance. Thanks are also due to Leadership Group members Bill Ury and Shamil Idriss, who facilitated highly productive

Group meetings and also offered many constructive comments on the Leadership Group Report.

The project has benefited from the wise counsel of numerous advisors. We thank Mark McKinnon, Vice Chairman of Public Strategies, Inc., and Mike McCurry, of Public Strategies Washington, Inc., for multiple consultations and their presentation at our June 2007 Leadership Group meeting. Former U.S. Representative and White House Chief of Staff Leon E. Panetta has lent both his wisdom and his endorsement. We also offer thanks to Richard Murphy, former Ambassador to Saudi Arabia and Assistant Secretary of State for Near East and South Asian Affairs, as well as Eboo Patel, founder of the Interfaith Youth Core, for their advice. Members of the Alliance for Peacebuilding provided guidance in the early stages of the project's development and we thank, in particular, Susan Hackley and Joseph Montville for their advice and support.

In addition, we thank the many dozens of people who provided thoughtful input and encouragement on the Leadership Group Report, especially those who attended our outreach and consultation meetings in Washington, DC, New York and Boston. Special thanks go to: Dennis Ross, Zack Snyder and the Washington Institute for Near East Policy for organizing and hosting a meeting with foreign policy and security analysts and scholars; Dan Christman, John Sullivan, Jerry Faber and the Institute for National Strategic Studies at the National Defense University for organizing and hosting a meeting with defense and military analysts; Ingrid Mattson, Dalia Mogahed, Ahmed Younis and the Gallup Organization for organizing and hosting a meeting with leaders of the Muslim-American community; Stephen Heintz for hosting and Gordon Goldstein for organizing a New York City meeting with members of the financial services community; and Nancy Kaufman for organizing and Sid Topol and Hal Belodoff for hosting two Boston meetings with Jewish and Muslim leaders.

Several organizations and individuals have collaborated with Search for Common Ground and the Consensus Building Institute in generating and reviewing public opinion analysis for this Report: Leadership Group member Dan Yankelovich, Heidi Gantwerk and Barbara Lee of the Viewpoint Learning organization; and Leadership Group members Dalia Mogahed and Ahmed Younis and the Gallup Organization.

We are grateful to a number of individuals and organizations for assistance with media and outreach strategy. Our thanks go to Richard Edelman, the CEO of Edelman, for the generous donation of media and communications services. Within Edelman, we extend our thanks to LG member Rob Rehg, Chris Hayes, Kathleen Reilly and Reid Porter. We thank Hewlett Foundation Communications Director Eric Brown for his advice and encouragement. We also want to acknowledge Rev. Robert Chase, Founding Director of Intersections, for bringing the USME Report to diverse religious communities.

One Nation: Liberty and Justice for All has provided generous in-kind support to the USME project by engaging Fenton Communications to build our project Web site. Special thanks go to Sharene Azimi of Fenton for overseeing this process. One Nation has also underwritten the work of Link TV to create a short documentary on this project. We are indebted to Wendy Hanamura, Lisa Aliferis and Souheila Al-Jadda of Link TV for their work.

We have been very fortunate in the generous and consistent financial support we have received from the Hewlett Foundation and the Rockefeller Brothers Fund. We gratefully acknowledge additional providers of substantial financial and in-kind support: Carnegie Corporation of New York; the American Petroleum Institute; the Bernard and Audre Rapoport Foundation; the W.K. Kellogg Foundation; the Financial Services Roundtable; Mr. George Russell; Dan Yankelovich; and Alan Yaffe. Invaluable donations have also been received from: the Small-Alper Family Foundation; the Divine-Triggs Joy Fund; Paul Guilden; Gretchen Sandles and Charles Hauss; Gary Jacobson; Ronna Stamm and Paul Lehman; the Deborah Zylberberg Porter Fund; the Topol Family Fund; Nancy Goldberg; the Steiner-King Foundation; Hugh and Donna Scott; Eugene "Jeep" Meyung; and other individual and institutional donors.

Finally, we want to acknowledge our colleagues at the two convening organizations for this project, Search for Common Ground (SFCG) and the Consensus Building Institute (CBI).

This project was nurtured from the beginning by the U.S. Consensus Council (USCC), an advisory group within SFCG. Several USCC members participated in the project's Leadership Group: Steve Bartlett, Stephen Heintz, and Dennis Ross. We thank other USCC members, former Senator Harris Wofford and Jessica Dibb, for their invaluable advice.

We would also like to acknowledge: SFCG Board Chairman George Moose and Board Member Dov Zakheim; SFCG Founder and President John Marks and Executive Vice President Susan Collin Marks; Leena El-Ali, director of the SFCG Partners in Humanity Project and Vanessa Arrington, an associate of that project; Tom Dunne, for his help in conceptualizing and coordinating the USME project; Senior Fellow Bill Belding; Senior Advisor Nancy Bearg (former National Security Advisor to the Vice President of the United States); staff member Junnaid Javed for his excellent research; Sara Willi, John Musselman and Anuradha Herath; and the dozens of interns, whose efforts were essential to the success of this endeavor.

Lauren Walters, Chairman of the Board of CBI, has provided exceptional guidance and support. CBI staff member David Hermann has provided exceptional assistance in research, writing, and analysis. Also from CBI, Andrew Maxfield and Sossi Aroyan have lent invaluable help.

Robert Fersh and David Fairman, Project Co-Directors
Paula Gutlove, Project Manager

Biographies of the Leadership Group Members

Madeleine Albright

Principal, The Albright Group LLC; former U.S. Secretary of State
WASHINGTON, DC

Madeleine Albright is a Principal of The Albright Group LLC, a global strategy firm, and Chair and Principal of Albright Capital Management LLC, an investment advisory firm focused on emerging markets. Dr. Albright was the 64th Secretary of State of the United States. In 1997, she was named the first female Secretary of State and became, at that time, the highest-ranking woman in the history of the U.S. government. As Secretary of State, Dr. Albright reinforced America's alliances, advocated democracy and human rights, and promoted American trade and business, labor, and environmental standards abroad. From 1993 to 1997, Dr. Albright served as the U.S. Permanent Representative to the United Nations and as a member of the President's Cabinet. She is the first Michael and Virginia Mortara Endowed Distinguished Professor in the Practice of Diplomacy at the Georgetown University School of

Foreign Service. She chairs both the National Democratic Institute for International Affairs, and the Pew Global Attitudes Project and serves as president of the Truman Scholarship Foundation. Dr. Albright co-chairs the UNDP's Commission on Legal Empowerment of the Poor, serves on the Board of Directors of the Council on Foreign Relations, the Board of Trustees for the Aspen Institute and the Board of Directors of the Center for a New American Security. Dr. Albright earned a B.A. with Honors from Wellesley College, and Master's and doctorate degrees from Columbia University's Department of Public Law and Government, as well as a Certificate from its Russian Institute. Dr. Albright is author of three New York Times bestsellers. Her autobiography, *Madam Secretary: A Memoir,* was published in 2003. In 2006, Dr. Albright published *The Mighty and the Almighty: Reflections on America, God, and World Affairs.* Her latest book, *Memo to the President Elect: How We Can Restore America's Reputation and Leadership* was published in January 2008.

Richard Armitage

President, Armitage International; former U.S. Deputy Secretary of State
WASHINGTON, DC

Richard Armitage is President of Armitage International L.C. He also serves on the Board of Directors of ConocoPhillips, ManTech International Corporation and Transcu Ltd., and is a member of The American Academy of Diplomacy and of the Board of Trustees of the Center for Strategic and International Studies. From 2001 to 2005, he served as Deputy Secretary of State. Previously, he was President of Armitage Associates L.C. since 1993. He was engaged in a range of worldwide business and public policy endeavors as well as frequent public speaking and writing. From 1992 to 1993, Mr. Armitage (with the personal rank of Ambassador) directed U.S. assistance to the new independent states (NIS) of the former Soviet Union, after having filled key diplomatic positions as Presidential Special Negotiator for the Philippines Military Bases Agreement and Special Mediator for Water in the Middle East, and Special Emissary to Jordan's King Hussein during the 1991 Gulf War. Earlier in his career, he served as Assistant Secretary of Defense for International Security Affairs and senior advisor to the 1980 Reagan presidential campaign. Mr. Armitage is a graduate of the U.S. Naval Academy and completed three combat tours in Vietnam. He is the recipient of numerous U.S. and foreign military decorations and public service awards, including the Presidential Citizens Medal, and a Knight Commander of the Order of St. Michael and St. George.

Ziad Asali

President and Founder, American Task Force on Palestine
WASHINGTON, DC

Ziad Asali, M.D., is the President and founder of the American Task Force on Palestine. Dr. Asali has been a long-time activist on Middle East issues. He has been a member of the Chairman's Council of American-Arab Anti-Discrimination Committee (ADC) since 1982, and served as ADC's President from 2001 to 2003. He was President of the Arab-American University Graduates from 1993 to 1995, and Chairman of the American Committee on Jerusalem, which he co-founded, from 1995 to 2003. Dr. Asali is also a Diplomat of the Board of Internal Medicine and a Fellow of the American College of Physicians. Dr. Asali has testified before the Senate on Palestinian education issues, and he has also testified at a hearing before the full U.S. House Committee on International Relations on the topic of "The Way Forward in the Middle East Peace Process." He served as a member of the United States official delegation to observe the Palestinian Presidential elections in January 2005. He also was a delegate with the National Democratic Institute to monitor the Palestinian Legislative election in January 2006.

Steve Bartlett

President and Chief Executive Officer, Financial Services Roundtable;
former U.S. Representative; former Mayor of Dallas, Texas
WASHINGTON, DC

Steve Bartlett is President of the Financial Services Roundtable. He served as a U.S. Representative from Texas' 3rd District from 1983 until 1991, and served as Mayor of Dallas from 1991 to 1995. Following his government service, Mr. Bartlett has sat on a number of Boards of Directors, including IMCO Recycling, Kaufman and Broad Home Corporation, Sun Coast Industrial and the YMCA of Metropolitan Washington. In addition, he has also served on the Board of Governors of the National YMCA, the Fannie Mae National Advisory Council and the Dallas-Fort Worth International Airport. He is currently Chairman of Easter Seals of Washington, Maryland, and Northern Virginia. He graduated with a B.A. from the University of Texas, Austin, later serving as an adjunct professor and guest lecturer at the LBJ School of Public Affairs.

Paul Brest

President, The William and Flora Hewlett Foundation
MENLO PARK, CA

Paul Brest is the President of the William and Flora Hewlett Foundation in Menlo Park, California. Mr. Brest received an A.B. from Swarthmore College in 1962 and an LL.B. from Harvard Law School in 1965. He served as law clerk to Judge Bailey Aldrich and Supreme Court Justice John M. Harlan, and practiced with the NAACP Legal Defense and Educational Fund, Inc., in Jackson, Mississippi, doing civil rights litigation before joining the Stanford Law School faculty in 1969, where his research and teaching focused on constitutional law, problem solving, and decision making. From 1987 to 1999, he served as the Dean of Stanford Law School. Mr. Brest is co-author of *Processes of Constitutional Decisionmaking* (4th ed. 2000), and currently teaches a law school course on Problem Solving, Decision Making, and Professional Judgment. He holds honorary degrees from Northeastern Law School and Swarthmore College, and is a member of the American Academy of Arts and Sciences.

Red Cavaney

President and Chief Executive Officer, American Petroleum Institute
ALEXANDRIA, VA

In addition to heading the American Petroleum Institute, Red Cavaney is the current Director of The United States Energy Association and Buckeye Technologies, Inc., and former Director of the Boards of the U.S. Chamber of Commerce and the National Association of Manufacturers, among others. Cavaney was President and CEO of the American Plastics Council, the American Forest and Paper Association, and the American Paper Institute before joining API in 1997. Earlier, he served as President and CEO of Irvine, CA-based Ericson Yachts and, in 1997, he was named Association Executive of the Year by Association Trends magazine and earned his Certified Association Executive (CAE) designation. He received the 2005 Bryce Harlow Foundation Business-Government Relations Award and the 2006 American Society of Association Executives (ASAE) Key Award. He has served as Chairman of ASAE and of the Associations Division of the U.S. Chamber of Commerce, in addition to sitting on the Board of Trustees of the Gerald R. Ford Foundation and the Center for Excellence in Education. He was a senior member of the White House staffs of U.S. Presidents Richard Nixon, Gerald Ford and Ronald Reagan. He is a 1964 NROTC graduate in Economics and History from the University of Southern California, served three tours of combat duty in Vietnam and was honorably discharged with the rank of U.S. Navy Lieutenant in 1969.

Daniel Christman

Lt. General (ret.), U.S. Army; Senior Vice President for International Affairs, U.S. Chamber of Commerce
WASHINGTON, DC

As Senior Vice President for International Affairs, Daniel Christman is responsible for representing the U.S. Chamber of Commerce before foreign business leaders and government officials and for providing strategic leadership on international issues affecting the business community. A career military officer, Dan served five years as the Superintendent of the U.S. Military Academy at West Point and also served for two years as the assistant to the Chairman of the Joint Chiefs of Staff, during which time he traveled with and advised Secretary of State Warren Christopher. He was centrally involved during this period with negotiations between

Israel and Syria as a member of the Secretary's Middle East Peace Team. Further, Dan represented the U.S. as a member of NATO's Military Committee in Brussels, Belgium. Graduating first in his class from West Point, Dan also received two Master's degrees from Princeton University and graduated with honors from the George Washington University Law School. He is a decorated combat veteran of Southern Asia, where he commanded a company in the 101st Airborne Division in 1969. On four occasions, he has been awarded the Army and Defense Distinguished Service Medal, the Department's highest peacetime award.

Stephen Covey

Co-Founder and Vice Chairman, FranklinCovey; writer, speaker, and academic
SALT LAKE CITY, UT

Stephen Covey is co-founder and Vice Chairman of FranklinCovey, the leading global professional services firm. FranklinCovey shares Dr. Covey's vision, discipline and passion to inspire, lift and provide tools for change and growth of individuals and organizations throughout the world. Dr. Covey is the author of several acclaimed books, including the international bestseller, *The 7 Habits of Highly Effective People*. It has sold more than 15 million copies in 38 languages throughout the world. Other bestsellers authored by Dr. Covey include *First Things First, Principle-Centered Leadership* and *The 7 Habits of Highly Effective Families*. Dr. Covey was recognized as one of Time magazine's 25 most influential Americans and one of Sales and Marketing Management's top 25 power brokers. Dr. Covey earned his undergraduate degree from the University of Utah, his MBA from Harvard, and completed his doctorate at Brigham Young University.

Thomas Dine

Principal, The Dine Group; former Executive Director, American Israel Public Affairs Committee
WASHINGTON, DC

Thomas Dine was Executive Director of the American Israel Public Affairs Committee (AIPAC). Most recently he was Chief Executive Officer of the Jewish Community Federation of San Francisco, the Peninsula, Marin and Sonoma Counties. Previously he was President of Radio Free Europe/Radio Liberty in Prague, a position he held for eight years. From 1993 to 1997, he served as the Assistant Administrator of Europe and Eurasia at USAID. Prior to these leadership posts, Dine worked as a foreign policy specialist in the U.S. Senate (1970 to 1980), was a senior fellow at the Brookings Institution and held three fellowships at Harvard's Kennedy School of Government. Early in his career, he served at the American Embassy in New Delhi, India, and as a Peace Corps volunteer in the Philippines. Dine has published widely in the press, as well as in specialized foreign policy journals, and has edited two books. He and his wife, Joan, have two grown children.

Marc Gopin

James H. Laue Professor of World Religions, Diplomacy and Conflict Resolution; Director, Center for World Religions, Diplomacy and Conflict Resolution, Institute for Conflict Analysis and Resolution, George Mason University

ARLINGTON, VA

Marc Gopin is James H. Laue Professor of World Religions, Diplomacy and Conflict Resolution, and he is the Director of the Center for World Religions, Diplomacy and Conflict Resolution at George Mason University's Institute for Conflict Analysis and Resolution. Dr. Gopin has lectured on conflict resolution in Switzerland, Ireland, India, Italy, and Israel, as well as at Harvard, Yale, Columbia, Princeton, and numerous other academic institutions. He has trained thousands of people worldwide in peacemaking strategies for complex conflicts in which religion and culture play a role. He conducts research on values dilemmas as they apply to international problems of globalization, clash of cultures, development, social justice and conflict. Dr. Gopin has engaged in back channel diplomacy with religious, political and military figures on both sides of conflicts, especially in the Arab-Israeli conflict. Dr. Gopin was ordained as a rabbi at Yeshiva University in 1983 and received a Ph.D. in religious ethics from Brandeis University in 1993.

Stephen Heintz

President, Rockefeller Brothers Fund
NEW YORK, NY

Now the President of the Rockefeller Brothers Fund (RBF), Stephen Heintz has held top leadership positions in both the non-profit and public sectors throughout his career. Until he joined the RBF in 2001, Mr. Heintz was Founding President of Dēmos: A Network for Ideas & Action. Dēmos is a new public policy research and advocacy organization working to enhance the vitality of American democracy and promote more broadly shared prosperity. Prior to founding Dēmos, Mr. Heintz served as Executive Vice President and Chief Operating Officer of the EastWest Institute (EWI), where he worked on issues of economic reform, civil society development, and international security. He has published articles in the International Herald Tribune, The Washington Post, The Wall Street Journal Europe and several books and journals. He is a Magna Cum Laude graduate of Yale University.

Shamil Idriss

Chairman of the Board, Soliya
NEW YORK, NY

Shamil Idriss is Chairman of the Board of Soliya, a non-profit organization that uses latest Web-conferencing technology to bridge the gap between university students in the Middle East, North Africa, Europe, and the United States. In addition to his work with Soliya, Mr. Idriss serves as the Deputy Director of the UN Alliance of Civilizations. The Alliance aims to advance an action-plan involving multilateral agencies, governments and civil society organizations to improve cross-cultural relations, with priority emphasis on relations between Western and predominantly Muslim societies. Previously, Mr. Idriss served as Senior Advisor to the World Economic Forum (WEF) where he established the "action track" of the Council of 100 Leaders: West-Islamic World Dialogue Initiative (C-100) and served on the Steering Committee for that initiative. He was appointed in 2005 to the WEF's

Young Global Leaders Forum. From 2000 to 2004, he served as Chief Operating Officer of Search for Common Ground, managing the organization's global operations and its headquarters in Washington, DC.

Daisy Khan

Executive Director, American Society for Muslim Advancement
NEW YORK, NY

Daisy Khan is Executive Director of the American Society for Muslim Advancement (ASMA), a New York-based non-profit dedicated to strengthening an expression of Islam based on cultural and religious harmony and building bridges between Muslims and the general public. At ASMA, she has led numerous interfaith events like the theater production Same Difference and the Cordoba Bread Fest banquet. She has launched two groundbreaking flagship programs: Muslim Leaders of Tomorrow, and Women's Islamic Initiative in Spirituality and Equity (WISE), global movements to empower youth and women within the global Muslim community. Khan regularly lectures around the globe and has appeared on numerous media outlets, including CNN, Al Jazeera, and BBC World's Doha Debates. She is a weekly columnist for the The Washington Post's "On Faith" and is frequently quoted in print publications such as Time, Newsweek, Chicago Tribune, and The New York Times. In recognition of her community work, she is the recipient of numerous awards, including the Interfaith Center's Award for Promoting Peace and Interfaith Understanding, Auburn Seminary's Lives of Commitment Award, the Annual Faith Leaders Award, and 21 Leaders for the 21st Century.

Derek Kirkland

Advisory Director, Investment Banking Division, Morgan Stanley
NEW YORK, NY

Derek Kirkland worked in the Financial Institution Group (FIG) at Morgan Stanley for 22 years, in New York, London and San Francisco, acting as co-head of the group from 2003 to 2007. FIG is the largest industry coverage group in the Investment Banking Division. Prior to joining Morgan Stanley in 1986, Derek was Director of Card Marketing at American Express (1984 to 1986) and a consultant at Booz Allen Hamilton (1982 to 1984). Derek holds a Master in Public Policy (MPP) degree from the John F. Kennedy School of Government at Harvard University, where he was a JFK Scholar in 1983, and a B.A. from Princeton University, from which he graduated Phi Beta Kappa and Summa Cum Laude in 1979. Currently a board member of The Hughes Foundation and the Progressive Book Club, Derek has been active on numerous charitable boards over the last decade. Derek is married to Lisa Hammersly, has three children and lives in New York City.

Richard Land

President, The Ethics & Religious Liberty Commission, Southern Baptist Convention; Member, U.S. Commission on International Religious Freedom

NASHVILLE, TN

Princeton and Oxford-educated, Dr. Richard Land has served as President of the Southern Baptist Convention's Ethics & Religious Liberty Commission since 1988. Dr. Land has represented evangelicals before Congress and U.S. presidents and as a commissioner of the U.S. Commission on International Religious Freedom. In 2005, Time named Dr. Land one of "The 25 Most Influential Evangelicals." He is the host of two nationally syndicated radio programs—"For Faith & Family" and "For Faith & Family's Insight"—and is the author of *Imagine! A God-Blessed America*. In 2006, Dr. Land was selected for membership in the Council on Foreign Relations, an independent, nonpartisan think tank and publisher with the mission "to better understand the world and the foreign policy choices facing the United States and other governments." A renowned scholar, Dr. Land has worked as a pastor, theologian, and public policy maker.

Robert Jay Lifton

Lecturer on Psychiatry, Harvard Medical School; author of Superpower Syndrome

CAMBRIDGE, MA

Robert Jay Lifton is Visiting Professor of Psychiatry at the Harvard Medical School and the Cambridge Health Alliance. Until recently he was Distinguished Professor of Psychiatry and Psychology, The City University of New York; at John Jay College of Criminal Justice and the Graduate School and University Center and the Mount Sinai Medical Center; and Director of The Center on Violence and Human Survival at John Jay College of Criminal Justice. He had previously held the Foundations' Fund Research Professorship of Psychiatry at Yale University for more than two decades. He has been particularly interested in the relationship between individual psychology and historical change, and in problems surrounding the extreme historical situations of our era. He has taken an active part in the formation of the new field of psychohistory. Since September 11, 2001, he has been studying Islamist apocalyptic violence and American responses to 9/11, including their own apocalyptic tendencies. Dr. Lifton is a prolific author; his more recent books include *Superpower Syndrome: America's Apocalyptic Confrontation with the World*; *Destroying the World to Save It: Aum Shinrikyo, Apocalyptic Violence, and the New Global Terrorism*; *Hiroshima in America: Fifty Years of Denial*; and *The Protean Self: Human Resilience in an Age of Fragmentation*.

Denis Madden

Auxiliary Bishop of Baltimore; former Associate Secretary General, Catholic Near East Welfare Association

BALTIMORE, MD

The Most Reverend Denis Madden is Auxiliary Bishop for the Archdiocese of Baltimore, a position he has held since 2005. Prior to that time, Bishop Madden served as Associate Secretary General of the Catholic Near East Welfare Association, whose main activities include assisting the Holy See, preparing church leadership, building social service institutions, promoting social development and fostering interfaith communication. From 1994 to 1996 Bishop Madden also served as the Director of the Pontifical Mission for Palestine office in Jerusalem. Prior to assuming these responsibilities, Msgr. Madden was one of the co-founders of the Accord Foundation, a humanitarian organization that has worked since 1988 in the West Bank and Gaza. He holds a Master's degree in psychology from Columbia University in New York and a Ph.D. in clinical psychology from the University of Notre Dame. In addition, Bishop Madden is a licensed clinical psychologist in Maryland and the District of Columbia, and has written numerous journal articles and chapters in books in the field of psychology.

John Marks

President and Founder, Search for Common Ground
WASHINGTON, DC

John Marks is President and founder of Search for Common Ground, an international conflict prevention NGO headquartered in Washington, DC and Brussels, with offices in 17 countries. He also founded and heads Common Ground Productions, which produces radio and television programming around the world to help prevent and transform conflict. He wrote and produced The Shape of the Future series of TV documentaries, which was aired simultaneously on Israeli, Palestinian, and Arab satellite television—something that had never been done before. Mr. Marks served as a Foreign Service officer in Washington, DC and Vietnam. A graduate of Cornell University, he also was a fellow at Harvard's Institute of Politics and a visiting scholar at Harvard Law School. He is a best-selling, award-winning author and in 2006 was awarded the Skoll Fellowship for Social Entrepreneurship.

Susan Collin Marks

Senior Vice President, Search for Common Ground; author of Watching the Wind: Conflict Resolution during South Africa's Transition to Democracy
WASHINGTON, DC

Susan Collin Marks is the senior vice president of Search for Common Ground (SFCG). She is a South African and served as a peacemaker during this country's transition from apartheid to democracy. Her book, *Watching the Wind: Conflict Resolution during South Africa's Transition to Democracy* (United States Institute of Peace, Washington, DC, 2000; Arabic edition, Dar Al Ahliah, Amman, 2004), details this era of historic change. Susan lived in Jerusalem from 2002 to 2004, co-directing SFCG's Middle East program. She is the founding editor of *Track Two*, a quarterly publication on community and political conflict resolution. She serves on numerous boards, including the Executive Committee of the World Economic Forum's Council of 100 Leaders on Western-Islamic World Dialogue and the Abraham Path Initiative established by Harvard Law School's Global Negotiation Project. Honors include a 1994/5 Jennings Randolph Peace Fellowship at the United States Institute of Peace, the Institute for Noetic Science's Creative Altruism award in 2005, and a Skoll Fellowship for Social Entrepreneurship in 2006. In 2006, she launched the Leadership Wisdom Initiative at SFCG offering leadership development and one-on-one support to political and civil society leaders. She speaks, teaches, coaches, mentors, writes, facilitates, and supports peacemakers, peace processes and conflict resolution programs internationally.

Ingrid Mattson

President, The Islamic Society of North America; Professor of Islamic Studies, Director of Islamic Chaplaincy, and Director, Duncan Black Macdonald Center for the Study of Islam and Christian-Muslim Relations, Hartford Seminary
HARTFORD, CT

In 2006 Ingrid Mattson was elected President of the Islamic Society of North America (ISNA) where she had previously served two terms as Vice President. Dr. Mattson was born in Canada and studied Philosophy at the University of Waterloo, Ontario (B.A., 1987). From 1987 to 1988 she lived in Pakistan where she worked with Afghan refugee women and she continued to work with Afghan women's groups after returning to the United States. Dr. Mattson earned her Ph.D. in Islamic Studies from the University of Chicago in 1999. She has written articles exploring the relationship between Islamic law and society, as well as gender and leadership issues in contemporary Muslim communities. Her book, *The Story of the Qur'an: Its History and Place in Muslim Societies* was published in 2007 by Blackwell Press. Dr. Mattson is frequently consulted by media, government and civic organizations and has served as an expert witness. She lives in Connecticut with her husband and children.

Sayyeda Mirza-Jafri

Strategic Philanthropy Consultant
NEW YORK, NY

Sayyeda Mirza-Jafri is a strategic philanthropy consultant. Most recently she was the Project Manager for One Nation: With Liberty and Justice for All whose mission is to reframe perceptions of Islam and Muslims in the American context. Prior to One Nation, Mrs. Mirza-Jafri was engaged in developing a Middle East and North Africa leadership program for the EastWest Institute. Mrs. Mirza-Jafri served as Program Associate for the Bridging Leadership Program at the Synergos Institute, where she managed a global network of partner organizations and organized and co-facilitated the global leadership trainings in Southern Africa, Latin America and Southeast Asia. Additionally, she has foreign policy work experience in several other organizations. At the Council on Foreign Relations, she focused on issues related to Islam and was involved in the project "Pluralism in Muslim Societies." At the Center for Strategic and International Studies she focused on the Middle East and North Africa. Mrs. Mirza-Jafri obtained a Master's degree in International Political Economy from the London School of Economics in 1999, focusing on issues of economic development, investment and political barriers in developing countries. She graduated cum laude from New York University with a B.A. in International Politics and Middle East Studies and her honors thesis focused on Islamic reformist feminist thought. Her language skills at various levels include Arabic, Bengali, Hindi, Persian, Spanish and Urdu.

Dalia Mogahed

Executive Director, Gallup Center for Muslim Studies; co-author with John Esposito of Who Speaks for Islam? What a Billion Muslims Really Think
WASHINGTON, DC

Dalia Mogahed is the Executive Director of the Gallup Center for Muslim Studies. With John L. Esposito, Ph.D., she is co-author of the book *Who Speaks for Islam? What a Billion Muslims Really Think*. Ms. Mogahed provides leadership, strategic direction, and consultation on the collection and analysis of Gallup's unprecedented surveying of more than one billion Muslims worldwide. She also leads the curriculum development of a three-day executive course on findings from The Gallup Poll of the Muslim World. Prior to joining Gallup, Ms. Mogahed was the founder and director of a cross-cultural consulting practice in the United States, which offered workshops, training programs, and one-to-one coaching on diversity and cultural understanding. Ms. Mogahed earned her Master's degree in business administration with an emphasis in strategy from the Joseph M. Katz Graduate School of Business at the University of Pittsburgh. She received her undergraduate degree in chemical engineering.

Vali Nasr

Professor of International Politics, The Fletcher School, Tufts University; Adjunct Senior Fellow for Middle Eastern Studies, Council on Foreign Relations

MEDFORD, MA

Vali Nasr is Professor of International Politics at The Fletcher School, Tufts University. He is also an Adjunct Senior Fellow for Middle Eastern Studies at the Council on Foreign Relations in New York. His areas of focus for research and teaching include Comparative Politics, International Political Economy, South Asia, Iran, the Middle East, and Political Islam. His work has been translated into Arabic, Indonesian, Turkish, Persian, Chinese, and Urdu. Dr. Nasr has been the recipient of grants from the John D. and Catherine T. MacArthur Foundation, The Harry Frank Guggenheim Foundation, Social Science Research Council, and the American Institute of Pakistan Studies. Dr. Nasr earned his degrees from the Massachusetts Institute of Technology (Ph.D., 1991), the Fletcher School of Law and Diplomacy (MALD, 1984), and Tufts University (B.A., 1983).

Feisal Abdul Rauf

Imam, Masjid al-Farah in New York City; Founder and Chairman, Cordoba Initiative; author of What's Right with Islam Is What's Right with America

NEW YORK, NY

Imam Feisal Abdul Rauf is Chairman of the Cordoba Initiative, an independent, international, interreligious project that works with state and non-state actors to improve Muslim-West relations. Author of *What's Right With Islam Is What's Right With America: A New Vision for Muslims and the West*, he is also founder and CEO of the American Society for Muslim Advancement (ASMA) and Imam of Masjid al-Farah. Imam Feisal is a member of the World Economic Forum Council of 100 Leaders on Western-Islamic World Dialogue and the recipient of The Alliance for International Conflict Prevention and Resolution's

Annual Alliance Peacebuilder Award and The Interfaith Center of New York's Annual James Park Morton Interfaith Award.

Rob Rehg

President, Washington, DC Office, Edelman
WASHINGTON, DC

Rob Rehg has worked in public relations, journalism, politics and public affairs for more than 25 years. He is also an adjunct professor for the University of Virginia's professional education program. For Edelman, Rob has managed rollout of reports for the 9/11 Commission and Iraq Study Group, crisis communications for the American Red Cross, and integrated educational advocacy programs for the nation's oil, freight rail and auto industries. His clients have included AT&T, Boeing, Business Roundtable, GE, Nissan, USAir, UNOCAL, British Petroleum, S.C. Johnson, Wal-Mart, and The Church of Jesus Christ of Latter-day Saints. His management of international clients includes work for the governments of Chile, Portugal, Korea, Malawi, Angola, India and government agencies such as the Panama Canal Authority. In addition to his work at Edelman, Rob has served as director of communications for the Archdiocese of Baltimore. In the realm of politics, he was chief of staff for Michigan Rep. Bill Schuette and director of communications and policy for Michigan Rep. Dave Camp. As a journalist, Rob worked as a congressional correspondent for Hearst Newspapers' Washington Bureau, writing for newspapers in San Francisco, Los Angeles, Seattle, New York, Texas, Michigan, Illinois and Florida. Prior to joining the Washington Bureau, Rob was an editor, political columnist and reporter for Hearst Newspapers in Michigan and Illinois, and a radio reporter for stations in St. Louis, Missouri.

Dennis Ross

Consultant, Washington Institute for Near East Policy; former U.S. Special Middle East Envoy and Negotiator
WASHINGTON, DC

Dennis Ross is currently a consultant for the Washington Institute for Near East Policy. A highly skilled diplomat, Ambassador Ross was the U.S. point man on the Middle East peace process in both the George H. W. Bush and Bill Clinton administrations. Instrumental in assisting Israelis and Palestinians to reach the 1995 Interim Agreement, he also successfully brokered the 1997 Hebron Accord, facilitated the 1994 Israel-Jordan peace treaty, and intensively worked to bring Israel and Syria together. A scholar and diplomat with more than two decades of experience in Soviet and Middle East policy, Ambassador Ross worked closely with Secretaries of State James Baker, Warren Christopher, and Madeleine Albright. Since leaving government in 2001, he is widely published and a frequent contributor to the Financial Times, The Washington Post, Los Angeles Times, and U.S. News and World Report, as well as a foreign affairs analyst for the Fox News Channel. Ambassador Ross is the author of *The Missing Peace: The Inside Story of the Fight for Middle East Peace.*

S. Abdallah Schleifer

Distinguished Professor of Journalism, American University in Cairo; former Washington Bureau Chief, Al Arabiya news channel; former NBC News Cairo bureau chief
PHILADEPHIA, PA

S. Abdallah Schleifer, Distinguished Professor of Journalism and Mass Communication at the American University in Cairo (where he founded and served as the first director of the Kamal Adham Center for Journalism Training and Research), is a veteran journalist who has covered the Middle East for American and Arab media for more than 40 years. He served as NBC News bureau chief in Cairo, as an NBC news producer-reporter based in Beirut, as Middle East correspondent for Jeune Afrique, and as a special correspondent of the New York Times in Amman, Jordan and the Israeli-occupied territories. A frequent contributor of articles on mass media as well as Arab and Islamic affairs to scholarly and specialist journals, Prof. Schleifer is an Adjunct Scholar at the Middle East Institute in Washington, DC, a Senior Fellow at the Royal Aal al Bayt Institute for Islamic Thought in Amman, Jordan, and a Senior Fellow at the Foreign Policy Research Institute in Philadelphia. He was a Visiting Scholar at St. Antony's College at Oxford (2006 to 2007) and served on the International Advisory Board of the World Media Association. Prof. Schleifer's controversial book *The Fall of Jerusalem*, which is an eyewitness account of the 1967 Arab-Israeli War, received critical acclaim in the mid-1970s. A graduate of the University of Pennsylvania (B.A., 1956), Prof. Schleifer received his M.A. from the American University of Beirut in Islamic Political Thought in 1980.

Jessica Stern

Lecturer in Public Policy, Harvard Kennedy School of Government
CAMBRIDGE, MA

Jessica Stern is the Academic Director of the Program on Terrorism and the Law at Harvard Law School and a Lecturer in Government at Harvard University, where she teaches courses on terrorism and counterterrorism. She is the author of *Terror in the Name of God: Why Religious Militants Kill*, and *The Ultimate Terrorists*, as well as numerous articles. She served on President Clinton's National Security Council Staff and was selected by Time magazine in 2001 as one of seven thinkers whose innovative ideas "will change the world." Stern advises a number of government agencies and has taught courses for government officials, and she was an analyst at Lawrence Livermore National Laboratory. She was recognized by FBI Director Robert Mueller for her assistance to the U.S. government in its effort to thwart international terrorism. She has served on the Advisory Boards of various organizations, and currently serves on the editorial boards of Current History and Bulletin of the Atomic Scientists, and is a member of the Trilateral Commission. Stern has been named a fellow at the Council on Foreign Relations, Stanford's Hoover Institution, the World Economic Forum, and Harvard. She has a bachelor's degree from Barnard College in chemistry, a Master's degree from MIT in technology policy, and a doctorate from Harvard in public policy.

Mustapha Tlili

Director, Center for Dialogues: Islamic World-U.S.-The West, New York University
NEW YORK, NY

Mustapha Tlili has taught at Columbia University's School of International and Public Affairs and was a Senior Fellow at the World Policy Institute of New School University and Director of its UN Project. He is a former senior UN official, having served as Director for Communications Policy in the United Nations Department of Public Information, Director of the UN Information Centre for France, and Chief of the Namibia, Anti-Apartheid, Palestine and decolonization programs in the same department. An established novelist, Mustapha Tlili is a Knight of the French Order of Arts and Letters. In addition, he edited and contributed to *For Nelson Mandela* (Henry Holt, 1987) and published an essay on Machiavelli's Theory of Government in the Sorbonne's *Revue de Métaphysique et de la Morale*. Mustapha Tlili is a member of Human Rights Watch's Advisory Committee for the Middle East and North Africa.

William Ury

Co-Founder, Program on Negotiation, Harvard Law School; co-author of Getting to Yes
BOULDER, CO

William Ury is co-founder of the Program on Negotiation at Harvard Law School, where he directs the Global Negotiation Project. He is co-author of the international bestseller *Getting to Yes* and author of *Getting*

Past No and *The Third Side*. Over the last twenty-five years, Dr. Ury has mediated between quarrelling corporate divisions, battling unions and management, and warring ethnic groups around the world. He has also served as a negotiation consultant to governments and dozens of Fortune 500 companies. Dr. Ury is co-founder of the e-Parliament, a problem-solving forum and ideas bank for effective legislation, connecting members of congresses and parliaments around the world. His most recent project is the Abraham Path Initiative, which seeks to create a permanent path of tourism and pilgrimage in the Middle East that retraces the footsteps of Abraham, the unifying figure of Judaism, Christianity, and Islam. Trained as an anthropologist, Dr. Ury holds a B.A. from Yale and a Ph.D. from Harvard.

Vin Weber

Managing Partner, Clark and Weinstock; Chairman, National Endowment for Democracy; former U.S. Representative
WASHINGTON, DC

Vin Weber is Managing Partner of Clark & Weinstock's Washington office. Mr. Weber provides strategic advice to institutions with matters before the legislative and executive branches of the Federal government. Mr. Weber is also Chairman of the National Endowment for Democracy, a private, non-profit organization designed to strengthen democratic institutions around the world through nongovernmental efforts. He is a Senior Fellow at the Humphrey Institute at the University of Minnesota. Mr. Weber is a board member of several private sector and non-profit organizations, including ITT Educational Services, Department 56, and the Aspen Institute. He also serves on the board of the Council on Foreign Relations and co-chaired a major independent task force on U.S. Policy Toward Reform in the Arab World with former U.S. Secretary of State Madeleine Albright. Mr. Weber served in the United States House of Representatives from 1981 to 1993, representing Minnesota's 2nd Congressional District. He was a member of the Appropriations Committee and an elected member of the House Republican Leadership.

Daniel Yankelovich

Founder and Chairman, Public Agenda; author
LA JOLLA, CA

Named by PR Week as among the ten most influential people of the past century in the arena of public affairs, communications, and public relations, Daniel Yankelovich has spent a half century monitoring social change and public opinion in America. In the 1970s and 1980s he initiated the New York Times/Yankelovich poll, founded (with Cyrus Vance) Public Agenda—a non-partisan not-for-profit public policy research organization—and established DYG Inc., a firm that tracks social and market trends. After moving to California in the 1990s, he founded his newest firm, Viewpoint Learning, which specializes in dialogue-based learning. He is director emeritus of CBS, US West, the Meredith Corporation, Diversified Energies, Loral Space and Communications and ARKLA and trustee emeritus of Brown University, the Kettering Foundation, the Fund for the City of New York and the Educational Testing Service (ETS), where he also served as Chairman of the Board. He is a member of the American Academy of Arts and Sciences and the Council on Foreign Relations, where he served on the membership committee and contributed articles to Foreign Affairs. He is the author of eleven books including *Profit With Honor: The New Stage of Market Capitalism, Coming to Public Judgment: Making Democracy Work in a Complex World*, and *The Magic of Dialogue: Transforming Conflict into Cooperation.*

Ahmed Younis

Senior Analyst, Gallup Center for Muslim Studies; former National Director, Muslim Public Affairs Committee
WASHINGTON, DC

A graduate of Washington & Lee School of Law, Ahmed Younis is an expert on American Muslims and other topics such as terrorist financing, public diplomacy, identity/integration and issues affecting the relationship between the global Muslim Community and the West. He served as National Director of the Muslim Public Affairs Committee in Washington, DC from 2004 to 2007. He is the author of *American Muslims: Voir Dire (Speak the Truth)*, a post-September 11 look at the reality of debate surrounding American Muslims, their country and their integration. In 2006 Mr. Younis traveled on behalf of the Department of State to Turkmenistan, Tajikistan and Kyrgyzstan, where he met with government, community, and religious leaders, and visited madrassas across the region. He is a frequent guest on numerous television and radio shows and his work has been featured in several leading newspapers. Mr. Younis worked as an intern at the Office of the Legal Counsel of the Office of Legal Affairs of the United Nations. He has studied and lived in Egypt and Saudi Arabia and is fluent in Arabic.

Dov Zakheim

Vice President, Booz Allen Hamilton; former U.S. Under Secretary of Defense (Comptroller)
WASHINGTON, DC

Dov Zakheim is currently Vice President of Booz Allen Hamilton's global defense business. As a public servant, his previously held positions include Under Secretary of Defense (Comptroller) and CFO for the Department of Defense from 2001 to 2004, and Deputy Undersecretary of Defense for Planning and Resources from 1985 to 1987. He is a three-time recipient of the Department of Defense's highest civilian award, the Distinguished Public Service Medal, as well as other awards for government and community service. A 1970 graduate of Columbia University with a B.A. in government, he earned his doctorate in economics and politics at St. Antony's College, University of Oxford. Dr. Zakheim is a member of the Council on Foreign Relations, the International Institute for Strategic Studies, and the United States Naval Institute. The author of a dozen books and monographs and of numerous articles, Dr. Zakheim has lectured and provided print, radio and television commentary on national defense and foreign policy issues domestically and internationally.

Background on the U.S.-Muslim Engagement Project and the Convenors

1. The U.S.-Muslim Engagement Project

Search for Common Ground and the Consensus Building Institute, two non-profit organizations with expertise in building consensus on complex public issues, conceived, convened and staffed this project.

The project's goals are to:

- Create a coherent, broad-based and bipartisan strategy and set of recommendations to improve relations between the U.S. and the Muslim world; and

- Communicate and advocate this strategy in ways that shift U.S. public opinion and contribute to changes in U.S. policies, and public and private action.

In 2006, project staff interviewed scores of individuals who are knowledgeable about the key issues in U.S.-Muslim relations and whose views reflected a wide diversity of experience and political viewpoint. Nearly uniformly, those consulted supported the project's goals and proposed approach: to convene diverse leaders; facilitate frank, mutually respectful discussions among them to clarify both challenges and options for improving relations; ensure that the dialogue reflected not only elite perspectives, but also the views and values of citizens in the U.S. and in Muslim countries and communities; and ultimately produce a wise and broadly supportable strategy for improving U.S.-Muslim relations. The interviews also confirmed that no other organization was undertaking this mission, and that if successful, it could be of great value to the U.S., Muslim countries and communities, and the international community as a whole.

During this extensive outreach process, the staff team formed relationships with groups and individuals who were essential to the successful implementation of the project. The interviewing process was instrumental in the selection and formation of the diverse and eminent Leadership Group on U.S.-Muslim Engagement, which has deliberated for nearly two years to produce this Report.

The Leadership Group as a whole met face to face four times, in January 2007, July 2007, January 2008, and June 2008. The initial Summit, hosted by Rockefeller Brothers Fund at their Pocantico Conference Center, established a clear sense of shared mission and central themes to be included in this Report. It also served to build relationships and trust among the highly diverse Leadership Group. From that point forward, the Leadership Group, through a carefully facilitated dialogue process, worked with the project staff and representative groups of the American public to explore a wide range of issues. The Leadership Group also conducted outreach to key constituencies, and commissioned research on public opinion to test the viability of options for improving relations.

Through this process of research, analysis and deliberation, the Leadership Group has formed a clear and strong consensus on a strategy to enhance U.S. and international security by working more intensively and directly on the underlying causes of tension with key Muslim countries and communities. The strategy is described in this Report.

A key assumption of this project has been that building consensus on recommendations among a group of highly respected and diverse American leaders, informed by public opinion and input, could actually lead to changes in public and private action and to a more peaceful world—but only if the leaders and the project team developed a strong and effective education and outreach strategy to engage decision makers, opinion makers, and the public.

The release of *Changing Course: A New Direction for U.S. Relations with the Muslim World* is the first step in an outreach process designed to stimulate discussion and action on the Report by government and the private sector. Concurrently, the Report aims to foster citizen dialogue about its findings and to encourage grass-roots involvement in improving U.S.-Muslim relations. The U.S.-Muslim Engagement Project, through its Leadership Group, its supporters, and its staff, is committed to catalyzing action at all levels of society consistent with the Report's recommendations.

2. The Project Staff

Staff Leadership

Robert Fersh, USME Project Co-Director and Executive Director, Search for Common Ground-USA. Robert Fersh directs the U.S. division of Search for Common Ground, where his central focus is organizing and conducting policy consensus processes on issues of national importance. Most recently, he directed a project among key national stakeholders on Health Care Coverage for the Uninsured that concluded in 2007. Mr. Fersh has over 30 years experience in national public policy issues, having held senior positions in the Executive Branch, with three Congressional Committees, and as president of a leading national non-profit organization working to end hunger in the U.S. He holds an undergraduate degree in Industrial and Labor Relations from Cornell University and a law degree from Boston University.

David Fairman, USME Project Co-Director and Managing Director, Consensus Building Institute. David Fairman served as principal author of the USME Leadership Group Report, *Changing Course: A New Direction for U.S. Relations with the Muslim World.* For more than 20 years, he has facilitated consensus building and mediated resolution of public conflicts internationally and in the United States. He works on national development plans with the United Nations Development Group, on complex projects with the World Bank Group, and on building public conflict resolution capacity with aid agencies, developing country governments and civil society organizations. He is Associate Director of the MIT-Harvard Public Disputes Program, a founding board member of the Alliance for Peacebuilding, and a member of the Council on Foreign Relations. He holds a Ph.D. in political science from MIT, and a B.A. from Harvard College.

Paula Gutlove, USME Project Manager and Deputy Director, Institute for Resource and Security Studies. Paula Gutlove has over 25 years of experience working with people of diverse perspectives and interests, to improve communication, build understanding, resolve conflicts, and promote cooperation. In 1996, she founded the Health Bridges for Peace project, which links health care with the prevention and resolution of inter-communal conflict in the Balkans, the Caucasus, the Middle East, and elsewhere. Dr. Gutlove is a founding board member and board chair of the Alliance for Peacebuilding, an Associate of the MIT-Harvard Public Disputes Program, and consultant to numerous international organizations. She holds a D.M.D. from Boston University and a B.S. from Cornell University, and has had post-doctoral fellowships in peace and conflict studies at Harvard University and the Australian National University.

Program Staff

Nancy Bearg, Senior Advisor, Search for Common Ground-USA

William Belding, Senior Fellow, Search for Common Ground-USA

Tom Dunne, Senior Project Manager, Search for Common Ground-USA

Leena El-Ali, Director, Partners in Humanity: For Constructive & Vibrant Muslim-Western Relations, Search for Common Ground

Anuradha Herath, Communications Fellow, Search for Common Ground-USA

David Hermann, USME Project Research Coordinator and International Programs Associate, Consensus Building Institute

Junnaid Javed, Research Fellow, Search for Common Ground-USA

John Musselman, Project Administrator, Search for Common Ground-USA

Additional Staff Members

Sossi Aroyan, Office Manager, Consensus Building Institute

Andrew Maxfield, Executive Assistant and Marketing Coordinator, Consensus Building Institute

Sara Willi, Executive Assistant, Search for Common Ground-USA

3. The Convening Organizations

Search for Common Ground

Founded in 1982, Search for Common Ground (SFCG) is a not-for-profit organization that works in seventeen countries to transform the way the world deals with conflict - away from adversarial approaches and towards collaborative problem solving. Over the past 26 years,

SFCG has identified underlying principles for dealing with conflict constructively:

- Conflict is both normal and resolvable

- Conflict can be transformed

- Peace is a process

- Humankind is interdependent

SFCG has developed a broad array of operational methods, which are collectively called the "toolbox." These methods include well-known conflict resolution techniques, such as mediation and facilitation, and less traditional ones, like TV productions, radio soap opera and community organizing.

The U.S.-Muslim Engagement Project has been conducted by Search for Common Ground-USA, the program of SFCG that works in the U.S. SFCG-USA focuses primarily on building consensus on recommendations among key stakeholders on issues of national importance. The work of SFCG-USA is guided by an eminent advisory group known as the U.S. Consensus Council. Several members of the U.S. Consensus Council have been deeply involved in the U.S.-Muslim Engagement Project.

Consensus Building Institute

The Consensus Building Institute (CBI) is a not-for-profit organization created by leading practitioners and theory builders in the fields of negotiation and dispute resolution. CBI works with leaders, advocates, experts, and communities to promote effective negotiations, build consensus, and resolve conflicts.

CBI improves the way that leaders use negotiations to make organizational decisions, achieve agreements, and manage multi-party conflicts and planning efforts. CBI uses proven principles, processes and techniques that improve group decision making on complex public and organizational issues. Many of these strategies have been developed through the Program on Negotiation and MIT-Harvard Public

Disputes Program at Harvard Law School, where a number of CBI's staff and Board members are affiliated.

CBI's managing directors are David Fairman and Patrick Field, who are experts in consensus building and negotiation theory and practice. CBI staff are senior professionals who provide training, facilitation, mediation, assessment and research services to clients on local, national, and international negotiations and collaborations. CBI also works with well-known senior partners and consultants who further expand its areas of expertise and capability. CBI professionals engage diverse stakeholders and assist them to identify shared goals, manage conflicts, and build productive working relationships in which participants achieve their goals and more.

4. Additional Resources on the Project Web site

A project Web site has been set up at www.usmuslimengagement.org. It features up-to-date information on project activities and events, including press releases, reviews and endorsements of the Leadership Group Report. It also provides additional information on the issues addressed in the Report:

- Listings of publications, both online and in print, by members of the Leadership Group

- Related initiatives on U.S. relations with Muslim countries and communities

- A video documentary on the U.S.-Muslim Engagement Project that has been produced by Link TV, whose mission is to provide programming that offers a unique perspective on international news, contemporary issues and various cultures around the world

- A Citizen Dialogue Kit (CDK) that provides a framework and a guide for citizen discussion of issues addressed in the Leadership Group Report. It is intended for community leaders, their representatives, and a range of organizations at all levels. The CDK enables them to conduct a 2-3 hour "mini-dialogue" in which people can learn more about the issues and the options for action, and can develop implementation strategies in which they can engage.

Index